"Dwight Mason provides encouragem[...] feels ordinary. His life, and the lives o[...] site church he leads, documents the 'c[...] expect when he or she works with God to rewrite their story."
—John C. Maxwell, author and speaker

"I've studied, taught, and written on the issues of leadership and influence for decades—and Dwight Mason nails them both in this book. *Only God: Change Your Story, Change the World* lays out a compelling, practical plan to make something of your life. . .by cooperating with God to write, as Dwight says it, 'bigger and better stories' than you ever could on your own."
—Pat Williams, Orlando Magic senior vice president and author of *Leadership Excellence*

"God gives you the freedom to write your own life story but invites you to let Him be the ultimate Author. Dwight Mason offers practical and biblical insights in his book *Only God: Change Your Story, Change the World*, where you will find encouragement to live your life to its fullest and best!"
—Dan Reiland, executive pastor at 12Stone Church, and author of *Amplified Leadership*

"This is a book chock full of stories that fire the imagination, alter perceptions, and reignite hope. . . . [*Only God*] helps readers experience their own stories more vividly and offers assurance that life-changing stories can be written by individuals, families, and groups. The book's authenticity begins with God's story and nestles each individual narrative into that unshakeable reality."
—Donald N. Bastian, bishop emeritus of the Free Methodist Church, author, and speaker

"This book is a must-read for anyone who needs a faith lift! As I read its pages, I was reminded that we serve a God who loves the word 'impossible' as well as one who still specializes in miracles."
—Stan Toler, bestselling author of more than eighty books, including *The Secret Blend*

"We all have an idea of what we want our lives to look like. The truth is that God's plan for your story is bigger and better than anything you could have imagined! Check out this book and see how God wants to begin to change your story right now."
—Greg Surratt, lead pastor at Seacoast Church, author of *Ir-Rev-Rend*

"Dwight Mason knows the power of a great story. And now, he's given us a book on how we can build a 'life story' which can have a compounding impact on the lives of people we touch every single day. As you read *Only God: Change Your Story, Change the World*, have your notepad or laptop near. You're going to want to take some notes on how 'your story' can change 'your world.'"
—John D. Hull, president / CEO EQUIP Leadership, Inc.

"This book is an excellent resource for anyone who desires to make an impact for God. Dwight Mason has written a work that is rich in wisdom, balanced in scripture, full in scope, and useful for anyone who has the desire to see his/her story become all that God has designed it to be. It will surely serve as a guidebook for many to accomplish great things for God."
—Richard Reising, author and speaker on church growth and health, president of Artistry Labs

Only

GOD

Special thanks: to Leonard Sweet for his permission to quote "A Magna Carta of Trust by an Out-of-Control Disciple" from his book *Soul Café*; also to Dr. Robert Clinton, for his permission to include leadership characteristics from *Clinton Leadership Commentary*, Volume 1, copyright 1999; to Peter Scazzero, for his permission to share some concepts from his book *Emotionally Healthy Spirituality*; to Neil T. Anderson, for his permission to use material from his *Victory over the Darkness*, pp. 38–39. Copyright 2000, Gospel Light/Regal Books, Ventura, CA 93003. Used by permission; and Danny Cox, for his permission to use his "Declaration of Personal Responsibility."

Scripture quotations marked NIV are taken from the HOLY BIBLE, NEW INTERNATIONAL VERSION®. NIV®. Copyright © 1973, 1978, 1984, 2011 by Biblica, Inc.™ Used by permission. All rights reserved worldwide.

Scripture quotations marked KJV are taken from the King James Version of the Bible.

Scripture quotations marked NKJV are taken from the New King James Version®. Copyright © 1982 by Thomas Nelson, Inc. Used by permission. All rights reserved.

Scripture quotations marked MSG are from *THE MESSAGE*. Copyright © by Eugene H. Peterson 1993, 1994, 1995, 1996, 2000, 2001, 2002. Used by permission of NavPress Publishing Group.

Scripture quotations marked NLT are taken from the *Holy Bible*. New Living Translation copyright© 1996, 2004, 2007 by Tyndale House Foundation. Used by permission of Tyndale House Publishers, Inc. Carol Stream, Illinois 60188. All rights reserved.

Scripture quotations marked NCV are taken from the New Century Version of the Bible, copyright © 2005 by Thomas Nelson, Inc. Used by permission. All rights reserved.

Scripture quotations marked NASB are taken from the New American Standard Bible, © 1960, 1962, 1963, 1968, 1971, 1972, 1973, 1975, 1977, 1995 by The Lockman Foundation. Used by permission.

Scripture marked GNT taken from the Good News Translation® (Today's English Standard Version, Second Edition), Copyright © 1992 American Bible Society. All rights reserved.

Scripture quotations marked PHILLIPS are taken from The New Testament in Modern English, copyright © 1958, 1959, 1960 J.B. Phillips and 1947, 1952, 1955, 1957 The Macmillian Company, New York. Used by permission. All rights reserved.

Scripture quotations marked CEB are taken from the Common English Bible ®. Copyright © 2011 by Christian Resources Development Corporation, Inc. Used by permission. All rights reserved.

Cover design: Dual Identity Inc., www.dualidentitydesign.com

Published by Barbour Publishing, Inc., P.O. Box 719, Uhrichsville, Ohio 44683, www.barbourbooks.com

Our mission is to publish and distribute inspirational products offering exceptional value and biblical encouragement to the masses.

Member of the
Evangelical Christian
Publishers Association

Printed in the United States of America.

Only

GOD

{ CHANGE YOUR STORY,
CHANGE *the* WORLD }

DWIGHT MASON
with
BRENDA MASON YOUNG

BARBOUR
PUBLISHING

Dedication

This book is gratefully dedicated to the three families
Only God could have given me.

- my wife Patty and our children
Caleb, Sarah, Jonathan, and Benjamin

- my dad and mom, James and Marie Mason;
my siblings Jean Potter, Brenda Young,
J. Mason, and their spouses and children

- the Newpointe Community Church family

I wake up every day thanking God for you and your
partnership in this grand adventure. Only eternity can
contain all the Only God moments we have shared.

Contents

{ Introduction }

I remember the day my brother and I got bunk beds. Ever since I had graduated from the crib, we shared a room *and* a big double bed. Shared jokes and comfort in the dark worked well until my leg took a crooked turn. From the knee down, the bone began growing at a right angle and became more pronounced each month. The doctors forecast a grim future for an active young boy full of athletic dreams. I would never be able to run, and I would need to wear a brace twenty-four hours a day just to be able to walk. That was the reason for the bunk beds.

Because the brace pinched my leg, I kicked restlessly all night long, so my poor brother was a bruised and battered bed buddy. I struggled with the brace even more in the daytime. It pinched my leg, prevented me from being fast and effective at play, and made me a misfit among other children.

That wasn't my only problem. I stuttered badly. I was a late bloomer with delayed speech. When I finally did talk, it was obvious that I couldn't do it confidently and clearly. Everyone tried to finish my stories and sentences for me. I usually just withdrew and tried not to attract any unnecessary attention to myself.

A dubious start for an athlete and public communicator.

But God changed my story and my world. I was surrounded by people who believed He could do the miraculous. And in response to the fervent, faithful prayers and active obedience of righteous people, He would do more than we could have thought or imagined. Godly people from our church joined my parents and grandparents in praying faithfully for God to do what only He could. After a time of extended prayer, in response to what he believed to be God's leading, my father removed the brace from my leg. We all watched in amazement as, over a period of months, my leg became straight and strong—without any medical intervention.

I was active enough to be a challenge to my parents and teachers and healthy enough to join the other boys in roughhousing and sports. I fulfilled my aspirations to be a high school athlete. In a story remarkable on its own, I played point guard for the Bible college basketball team that won the 1982 National Christian College Athletic Association regional tournament championship. I was named Most Valuable Player of the championship game, having set a record for assists that still stood on the thirtieth anniversary of that win. Today I remain active in sports and life in general.

Only God could change my story like that.

As I write this, I pastor an energetic and growing multisite church, where I speak to thousands weekly. I regularly engage business and church leaders in individual consultations and large group conferences. My speaking patterns still bear the traces of phonic struggles, and I have a difficult time sounding out new words. Mispronunciations come up from time to time, and in my circle of friends I am the "Yogi Berra" of wordsmithing. I don't let this shake my confidence but just do the best I can and speak with boldness, counting on God in my weakness to make me strong. Only God could heal my stammering tongue, embolden my timid spirit, and change my story like that.

A bit of my background story may make *Only God* more personal. In 1985, I moved to Sugarcreek, a beautiful village deep in the Amish heartland of Ohio that was settled by immigrants from Switzerland. Sugarcreek is still an intriguing blend of Swiss heritage and Amish culture mixed with contemporary American. It's a wonderful place to live, minister, and grow a family. I originally came here to pastor a little rural church that thrived and grew to become the NewPointe Community Church I pastor today. I married Patty Carson in 1989, and God has blessed our home with four children—Caleb, Sarah, Jonathan, and Benjamin.

I have discovered that every time you find a person who is a catalyst for change and impacts the world for good, you will also find many "only God" stories. When individuals cooperate with God to write bigger and better stories than they ever could on their own, God changes them so they can affect their world.

I am grateful for my new story. Even now, God is changing me so that the story He is writing through my life and circumstances will bring Him great glory, give me the satisfaction and fulfillment I crave, and change my world. What God has done and is doing for me is what He wants to do for every person. Join me on the change journey! When your obedience meets God's power, the story will be amazing.

That's what this book is all about. As you read through these pages, I want you to feel encouraged and challenged to write an "only God" story of your own.

As you make your way through this book, you'll read some amazing "only God" stories others— including myself—have written in their own lives. And you'll find some tips about how you can get started writing for yourself.

I know you have it in you to write an incredible "only God" story. I know that because I know that God has created you for greatness. He wants you to learn how to walk and talk and live in the kind of faith and obedience that can make you a world changer.

So get busy reading! Then get busy writing!

1

{ The Ultimate Author }

All the world's a stage,
And all the men and women merely players:
They have their exits and their entrances;
And one man in his time plays many parts.

William Shakespeare penned those words in his work *As You Like It*. With all due respect to the Bard of Avon, I believe the expanse of human history actually *is* an amazing story that God, the ultimate Author, has been writing—and is still writing today. But, unlike Shakespeare, I see men and women as God's partners and valued cocreators of the story, not as mere players acting out what has been scripted for them.

Each of us has a story that began without any choice on our parts. None of us had any input as to our gender, race, place of birth, class, parentage, or countless other elements provided at birth or in our formative years. But early on, we picked up the pen and began writing for ourselves through our choices.

All of us have written lines, pages, perhaps even whole chapters of life we wish we could just delete. The eleventh/twelfth-century Persian poet Omar Khayyam referred to the permanency of many of our choices when he wrote:

> *The Moving Finger writes; and, having writ,*
> *Moves on: nor all your Piety nor Wit*
> *Shall lure it back to cancel half a Line,*
> *Nor all your Tears wash out a Word of it.*

Knowing and cooperating with the One who began your story is essential for writing a positive adventure. A.W. Tozer said that your view of God is the most important thing about you. It influences everything else. An incomplete or false understanding of God's character and love will set the plot of your story in a dangerous direction. When you don't truly know God or walk in His wisdom, you will make poor choices and set negative consequences into motion. But understanding Him rightly sets you up for an epic adventure.

THE AUTHOR AS YOUR LOVING FATHER

Knowing and understanding God in a joyful, trusting way—the way He *wants* you to know and understand Him—is not an automatic byproduct of simple religious experience. In fact, I see two primary reasons for an all-too-common misunderstanding of God and His character among Christ followers.

First, an early shaping relationship with a parent or other authority may have been so harsh and short of God's design that it creates a distorted image of God, one that lasts into adulthood. One of the first men I mentored struggled with calling God "Father." Dan "loved Jesus," but he couldn't wrap his mind around talking intimately with and trusting anyone he pictured as an authority. That was because his biological father was distant, aloof, and neglectful. The personal experiences Dan did have with his father were often physically and verbally abusive. Sadly, his earthly father's character was also the character of the god Dan created in his mind. Of course, he didn't want *that* god taking any part in writing his story.

Second, some of us are more interested in what God can give us and do for us than we are in just knowing Him. We aren't interested in knowing Him or following His story line unless we believe it clearly goes in the direction we desire and provides us the things we want.

Both of those reasons have a common result: a lack of trust in God, our Father. If we didn't trust a distant, aloof, or abusive earthly father, then we'll have a very difficult time trusting in a loving heavenly Father who is anything but distant and aloof. The same holds true for a God whose plans, designs, and desires for us are often very different from our own.

But here's the good news: Jesus said that knowing the

truth sets us free. Knowing the truth about the character of the Author frees us to fully trust Him to help us write a story we did not design or even completely see.

I have a wonderful relationship with my dad. Sacrificing himself for me was his way of life. Dad provided for me without fail and was always available to meet my needs, even needs I didn't realize I had. His word was reliable, even when I couldn't understand why he asked certain things of me.

Trusting Dad when I didn't understand him or what he asked me to do was sometimes challenging. Eventually, however, I came to understand that when he asked me to do something, it was always because he loved me so much and wanted God's very best for me. That is why I trusted him and his loving wisdom.

Many years ago, I was engaged to a very attractive girl. I couldn't wait for our wedding day, but one month before we were to be married, Dad talked with me privately and asked me to consider postponing the wedding. He explained that he had seen some things in the one I loved that he believed would lead to hurt, perhaps even tragedy, if they were not handled before we were married. The lump in my throat and the ache in my heart were huge. I was afraid to lose her. But I had learned over many years the complete trustworthiness of my father's love and wisdom. My fear of going against his track record in my life was greater than my fear of losing my future plans to be married to this young woman.

As usual, Dad was right. When I postponed the wedding, I almost immediately saw a side of my fiancée that had been hidden. She stepped out on me. She broke my heart, revealing things about her character that would have been even more devastating down the road. Trusting my father's wisdom saved my story and helped make it great.

I know that not everyone's earthly father is as loving and wise as mine. But I also know that my heavenly Father is infinitely more wise than Dad—and that He wants men and women to live in His love and wisdom. The key to living in that love and wisdom is knowing some vital truths about the One I comfortably and confidently call "Father."

THREE WONDERFUL TRUTHS ABOUT GOD OUR FATHER

Three wonderful truths about God can transform our relationship with Him. . .when we choose to accept and embrace them. These truths are:

1. God is *great*. He has all the power and wisdom needed to do the miraculous in my life.

2. God is *good*. All His desires for me are for my benefit.

3. God is *generous*. His plan is to use His greatness and goodness to bless me.

It's amazing what these truths can do for the person who chooses to believe them. I am so convinced of my Father's greatness, goodness, and generosity that I live with the confidence that the phone can ring at any time with an opportunity or a resource to fulfill His purposes and my dreams. I believe that even when I face opposition in following His plans.

Here's just one of many examples of this truth in my own life:

A number of years ago, God put relocation of the church I pastor on my heart. I believed that moving was a part of His story for my life and for the congregation I pastor. However, it was *not* a popular idea with our leaders. When the congregation voted to relocate, we lost 90 percent of our board. All but one of the board members not only resigned from the board, but they left the church, some in disgust and anger. One of the men looked into my eyes across a breakfast table and told me, "I don't believe I have ever disliked a person as much as I dislike you."

Others simply didn't want to be involved in this story because they saw certain failure ahead. One frustrated board member stood in the church lobby the day of his final exit and shook his head. "How do you expect to pay for all of this?" he asked.

"Because I have total confidence in my Father," I answered sincerely, "that's not my problem. My job is doing my best to follow what God has put on our hearts."

Through our obedience, my great, good, and generous Father was writing a bigger story than I dreamed. The first month we were in our new building, a man I had never met sent a check for three-quarters of a million dollars to the office. When our overwhelmed and excited business administrator called me with the news, I told him to hold the check because I didn't know if it was real or a joke. I called the businessman who wrote the check and confirmed that it was indeed real. Over breakfast, he explained that he gave the money because he believed in what we were trying to do and whom we were trying to reach. (By the way, he still doesn't attend our church.)

God is still using this man to help write the story of our adventure. Several years later, he came back to me with the question, "What are you wanting to do that you do not have the resources to begin?"

If you deeply believe in a great, good, and generous Father who wants to use all He has to bless you, questions like that never catch you off guard. You believe that any moment could be the beginning of an opportunity to write a new chapter. So I immediately listed ten audacious goals. He said he would look them over and get back to me. Sure enough, this quality man provided the resources we needed to begin our dream of multisites.

When you are obedient to God's leading you can be sure He has people waiting in the wings to add to your story.

TRUST: OUR PART IN THE BARGAIN

The key to any significant relationship is trust. When a child doesn't trust his parent, he will think he knows best and ultimately choose his own way. But God urges us toward a different choice in our relationship with Him:

> *Trust in the LORD with all your heart*
> *and lean not on your own understanding;*
> *in all your ways submit to him, and he*
> *will make your paths straight.*
> PROVERBS 3:5–6 NIV

Your heart is the control center of all you are—your thoughts, your will, your emotions. It's where the story line of your life gets its direction. You will never be able to fully live out the epic adventure God has planned for you without completely trusting in Him with all your heart.

Trust is not an emotion. It's a choice that *affects* your emotions, but it begins as a solid, rational decision to choose God's wisdom over your own understanding. You then solidify that with ongoing ("in all your ways") submission to everything He says.

This is how the story becomes amazing and purposeful. When I genuinely trust God, He takes responsibility to make my paths straight, my story great. That's the simple and strong message of Proverbs 3:5–6.

Trusting God isn't always easy. As we partner with Him, things can happen that tempt us to go into the natural human default mode—mistrusting Him and trusting ourselves.

Back in the very early days of my leadership of the church in Sugarcreek, we had grown enough that I believed we needed to go to two Sunday services each week. The church body supported this direction, but the board overruled the decision. The board members believed going to two services would hurt the unity and direction of the church.

I was angry and frustrated. I went home and told my wife, Patty, "Pack your bags. We are not staying here." Dangerous words. In my disappointment, I had forgotten how trustworthy my Father is. I had lost sight of the fact that God has promised that when I am authoring my story with Him, He takes responsibility to work all things together for good (see Rom. 8:28). I was leaning on my own understanding, so I was setting the plot of my story in a dangerous direction.

God is so great, so good, and so generous that He will not allow anyone to ruin my life story but me. For that, I am so thankful. Within a few hours after announcing to Patty that we were moving, I had worked through my disappointment and decided to trust my Father's hand. Besides, it wasn't *my* church—it was *His* church—and He would take responsibility for anything and anyone submitted and surrendered to Him.

We can't always understand God, the way He works, or the events and elements He allows in our story. Isaiah 55:8–9 (NIV) says:

> *"For my thoughts are not your thoughts,*
> *neither are your ways my ways," declares*
> *the LORD. "As the heavens are higher than*
> *the earth, so are my ways higher than your*
> *ways and my thoughts than your thoughts."*

This writes in bold font and underscores our need to trust. Our intelligence and wisdom are limited, so we may not *understand* God and His ways. But our trust can be complete, because it is a choice, a decision of our will. The strength of our relationship with Him depends on it.

The truth is, you and I were created for adventure. We were made to partner with the ultimate Author and write a heroic, fearless, and noble account. The prophet Daniel wrote, "But the people that do know their God shall be strong, and do exploits" (Dan. 11:32 KJV).

When you know God the way He wants you to know Him, you will find it much easier to choose to trust His greatness, goodness, and generosity. That trust is the beginning of radical changes in your life. Partnering with Him to write a new story will change your life, and then the new you will change your world.

ACTION STEPS

1. Pray daily, "Father, help me truly know You and choose to trust You in all things."

2. Keep a journal with three sections: GREAT, GOOD, and GENEROUS. Every time you read a scripture, hear a story, or experience anything that affirms these characteristics of God, make a note.

2

{ God's Story }

Ever since God placed Adam and Eve in the Garden of Eden, He has been writing the greatest story line of all time.

The story of humankind was born in God's heart, and it has every element of a blockbuster tale. The story is simple but stunning. Recorded in the pages of the Bible and imprinted on the hearts of mankind through the centuries, it is the story of magnificent love given, spurned, and rejected. The story astonishes with an incredible turnaround made possible only through its hero's unimaginable sacrifice. It's the true account of how almighty God was willing to change *His* story so you and I could change *ours*.

In the first pages of the Bible, in the book of Genesis, we meet the story's *characters*. The first element of any great story, the characters are the ones who take action. God Himself, the great, good, and generous one, is the hero. His presence fills every page. We also meet the humans, His handmade creations—God's beloved children, created because He craved love and relationship. The hero only asks mankind to love Him in return—and to trust Him. We also meet God's enemy, Satan, the devil in serpent's clothing. Satan hates everything the Father loves, so he quickly becomes the humans' nemesis.

The *setting* of any story is the time and place where the action happens. God's story is unique in that there never was a time when He was not, so His story has no official "in the beginning." We start reading *before* time, when only God and His angels existed. We discover that at a point in time, eons ago in the story, the angelic forces became divided—the faithful and the fallen. The setting for humanity's story is right here on planet earth, in the universe God created specifically for humankind.

The *plot* is the third element of a superb story. Plot is defined as the events that make up a story, particularly as they relate to one another in a pattern or a sequence. The plotline is very direct and straightforward. God the Father wanted fellowship. His creative genius spoke into existence the splendor of the world as we know it. Filled with complex and intricate creations, the world was a marvel of supernatural design, and mankind was the magnificent centerpiece. Man was made just "a little lower than the angels" (Ps. 8:5 NIV). God's plan was for these humans He had created to love and trust Him, and in turn He would provide purpose and resources for them. God and humankind would develop a deep and fulfilling relationship, and together they would coauthor an ongoing story of joy and significance.

Conflict is the fourth literary element. Conflict is the struggle involving the main characters or ideas. The central character is on one side of the issue, and the struggle exists and magnifies as the other characters choose how they will relate to that main character—whether they will join forces or oppose him.

In God's story, Satan appears early. As he long ago rebelled and has been locked in eternal conflict with the Father, he is a sworn enemy to all targets of the Father's affection. Satan enters the garden with a single purpose— to alter the story. With malice and cunning, he deceives the man and woman God fashioned with such love. As they listen to Satan's twisted logic, they choose to trust their own wisdom instead of the faithful Father who has walked with them daily. They doubt that God has their very best interests at heart and choose to believe He would purposefully withhold from them things that would bless them. Adam and Eve *choose* to disobey Him and to look out for themselves. When they do, the story line shatters. Sin mars and scars the marvelous perfection of the creatures and the creation.

Rising out of the conflict is the element of *theme*, which is the central idea or belief of the story. In this story God is writing, His perspective is clear. He believes—no, He *knows*—that sin has broken the relationship between Himself and humankind. He also knows that humankind is broken but not worthless. At the moment of the first fatal sin, God does not allow the death of the perfection He created to be the final moment. He announces the theme of the rest of His story: He will send a Savior, a Redeemer, who will re-create broken people who place their trust in Him.

Since that moment in the garden, every son of Adam and every daughter of Eve has suffered brokenness. That theme is unwavering. But God kept His promise. Into our brokenness came Jesus, the perfect Son of God.

John 1:10–12 (NIV) summarizes this transforming theme:

> *He was in the world, and though the world*
> *was made through him, the world did not*
> *recognize him. He came to that which was*
> *his own, but his own did not receive him.*
> *Yet to all who did receive him, to those who*
> *believed in his name, he gave the right to*
> *become children of God.*

Can you imagine that? God rewrites His story so we can rewrite ours. From brokenness to a re-created child of God. Now that's a story!

Let me say it one more time—this re-creation happens when we *trust*. The entire Bible records God's redemptive story—God's immeasurable love, His intimate relationship with His creatures, the brokenness of sin, and the promised salvation fulfilled through Jesus. And then God's story developed and expanded through the obedient lives of trusting followers in every generation.

Now is the time for you to add your chapter.

TO BE CONTINUED. . .

There is an incredible final chapter coming for those who trust God. He has given us a preview of the triumphant finale to the earthbound part of His story, a story with no beginning or end. There is a time coming when all will be restored to the dominion and rule of Christ.

Looking forward to that time of story fulfilled, the apostle John wrote, "The kingdom of the world has become the kingdom of our Lord and of his Messiah, and he will reign for ever and ever" (Rev. 11:15 NIV).

The purpose and power rippling through that verse makes the hair on my arms stand on end. What a climax! A majestic conclusion to earth's story, which will usher in the part of the song and story that never ends, is just ahead for us.

Before almighty God fulfills that promise, however, He wants to empower us to live an awe-inspiring adventure. Jesus promised, "Very truly I tell you, whoever believes in me will do the works I have been doing, and they will do even greater things than these, because I am going to the Father" (John 14:12 NIV).

As you begin to change your story, God's goal is beyond your human comprehension. He wants your story to be full of those "greater things" of which He spoke so that you can bless and change the world around you. This is still God's story.

The only factor that can keep us from being blessed and passing on the blessing to the world around us is our own low level of faith. Jesus challenged, "According to your faith let it be done to you" (Matt. 9:29 NIV). There it is again—that critical trust issue. As we further God's story, our contribution depends on our trust.

HE NEVER PROMISED IT WOULD BE EASY

God's story doesn't edit out the difficult parts. It doesn't delete the seemingly tragic events. Prior characters in His story faced formidable giants, wept through long nights, and suffered the wrenching pain of loss.

As we read, we wait out the suspense, barely breathing, to see where the story goes. In God's story, trusting heroes always forge *through* tragedy, emerging stronger when the battle subsides. Generally, the greater the destiny, the greater the process is in getting there. When God allows your story to take a difficult twist, don't try to edit out the struggle or delete the conflict. Your character will grow stronger, your story more heroic, through difficulty as He fills in details you cannot yet see.

Joseph is one of God's most noble and recognizable characters (his story appears in the book of Genesis). His plot twists and turns. His story line includes so much intrigue that if God weren't telling it, it would be hard to believe. As we read Joseph's story, we wonder, *How could one man experience so many highs and lows?*

Here's what I'm talking about:

High: Joseph is his wealthy father's favorite son.
Low: His brothers hate him for it.

High: Joseph's dad gives him a beautiful robe.
Low: In a fit of jealous rage, his brothers sell him into slavery, which is a slightly better choice than they had originally planned—they *had* intended to kill him.

High: Joseph becomes lead slave in a wealthy household, and the master loves him.
Low: The master's wife "loves him" too much and has him falsely imprisoned for attempted rape when he refuses her lustful advances.

High: As a prisoner, Joseph distinguishes himself in multiple ways. He helps a fellow prisoner, who gratefully promises to remember Joseph and tell Pharaoh about him if he is ever released.
Low: The man is released and completely forgets Joseph for years.

High: When a troubled Pharaoh needs his dreams interpreted, the forgetful man finally remembers Joseph. Joseph had been right about the dreams that were shared in the prison. When Joseph is finally summoned, he correctly interprets Pharaoh's dream. He is subsequently released from prison and promoted to the second-highest position in the land.

Low: Joseph's plan to save Egypt from famine actually works, *but* it brings his cheating, murderous brothers to him.

High: Joseph chooses to forgive his brothers for their evildoing and ends up saving his own family. He also gets to see his elderly father again. Joseph provides a home for all of them, and the family is reunited.

Whew! Doesn't that leave you a little winded? You might be thinking, *Was all of that really necessary?* Yes, because God had a plan. Editing out a single one of those difficult chapters would have irreversibly altered the story. Joseph's cooperation, even when he didn't understand why all these things were happening to him, enabled him to write a story that has been retold for centuries and has inspired countless other heroic chapters in God's epic story of redemption. Joseph cooperated with God, and God did what only He could do. That cooperation changed Joseph's story, and his story changed the world.

You and I need to make a simple decision. No matter what, we will keep writing with God and let *Him* choose where the story goes. When we try to edit out or revise story lines because they require surrender or sacrifice—or because they bring pain—we risk missing the very thread that connects us to a grand adventure. And the pain of regret is far greater and lasts longer than the pain of sacrifice.

Considerable discussion has revolved around what scripture means when it says that after our earthly lives are concluded, God Himself will wipe away the tears from our eyes (see Rev. 21:4). Why are we crying? What is the meaning of those tears? I wonder if we will shed those tears when we realize how much more we could have done, how much bigger our story could have been, and how much more positive change we could have worked in the world had we trusted more deeply and obeyed more completely.

God's story is big, magnificent, noble, and heroic. It is beyond imagination. Isn't it mind boggling that He invites you to write with Him, to obey Him and allow Him to write a story He can use to amaze the world. . .

. . .no matter what has happened to you,

. . .no matter how old or young you are,

. . .no matter how miserably you have failed,

. . .no matter how broken you feel,

. . .no matter how hard you have already tried?

God can accomplish in five minutes with your willing, cooperative heart what you can't accomplish without Him in five years. All He asks is that you trust Him and write with Him.

God wrote into His story a world painted with more than ten million distinct colors. He created the leathery skinned hippopotamus, which weighs several tons, and the fragile Western pygmy blue butterfly, which has a dainty wingspan of half an inch—and He incredibly, exquisitely designed both for unique purposes. Knowing that, you can be absolutely sure that designer God did not create you, the height of His creation, for anything less than a purpose-filled, productive, and energized life.

You have a colossal chronicle in you, just waiting to be written. It's God's story. Join Him and write.

ACTION STEPS

1. Read the story of Joseph (Gen. 37–50). Highlight every time it says "the LORD was with Joseph." Note how many of these times God appeared to be anywhere *but* with Joseph.

2. Chart your life story, marking the major highs and lows. Meditate on those times and record the evidence from today's vantage point that God was always with you.

3

{ Understanding Your Story }

The Bourne Identity is a 1980 spy fiction novel by Robert Ludlum about an amnesiac who must discover who he is and why several groups, including the CIA, are trying to kill him. In one of the most memorable exchanges in the 2002 movie based on Ludlum's novel, Jason Bourne, the central character, shares with Marie, a young woman he meets in his search, that he doesn't understand the thoughts automatically springing to his mind. He is scanning sight lines, looking over his shoulder, noticing all the people around him. Marie reassures him that she does not see his thoughts as unusual. She reminds him that he has recently been shot, and people who have a traumatic experience frequently experience weird and confusing thoughts and emotions.

Still struggling and confused, Bourne says, "I can tell you the license plate numbers of all six cars outside. I can tell you that our waitress is left-handed and the guy sitting up at the counter weighs two hundred fifteen pounds and knows how to handle himself. I know the best place to look for a gun is the cab or the gray truck outside, and at this altitude, I can run flat out for a half mile before my hands start shaking. Now why would I know that? How can I know that and not know who I am?"

Ludlum says that quote resonates powerfully with moviegoers because, "we're all trying to find out who. . . we are, aren't we?"

Not all of us are trying to find out who we are, but we should be. If you don't understand your story (your life and influences to this point in your life), you don't understand who you are and why you do what you do. You have to understand your story to leverage all your resources for positive change.

THE IMPORTANCE OF KNOWING WHO YOU ARE

Christian history is filled with saints who understood the importance of knowing ourselves—and how self-knowledge relates to our knowledge of our heavenly Father. Here are just a few examples:

- Saint Augustine wrote in his *Confessions* (400 AD), "How can you draw close to God when you are far from your own self? Grant, Lord, that I may know myself that I may know Thee."
- In *The Way of Perfection*, Saint Teresa of Avila wrote, "Almost all problems in the spiritual

life stem from a lack of self-knowledge."

- John Calvin said, "Our wisdom...consists almost entirely of two parts: the knowledge of God and of ourselves."
- Paul the apostle wrote that we are to put off our old self, and put on the new self, created like God in righteousness and true holiness (Eph. 4:22–24).

Those statements may leave us overwhelmed and despairing because we know something isn't right. Consciously or unconsciously, we vicariously live out another person's desires or dreams, try so hard to fit in, and live our entire lives in a haze, unsure of who we are and why we are here.

Scores of songs and movie scripts record the frustrations of relationships where persons feel unknown and therefore not authentically loved.

That brings us to a vital question: How can we love ourselves as Jesus said if we don't even know who we are (Matt. 22:39)?

You come to saving faith by "surrendering" yourself to Jesus, but how can you surrender what you don't even know? You try your best to surrender, but several years later, not much has changed. You know you need change, but much of what you have been taught hasn't helped you become the person you want to be. The approaches to spiritual growth you were taught seemed helpful at one time, but you still struggle with many of the same things you wrestled with before you came to Christ. You know that followers of Jesus are supposed to be joyful and become more like Jesus, but you struggle to find joy in your relationship with God. So you end up wondering what is wrong with you.

Our perceptions of self are shaped very early through the reactions and perceptions of others. When their perceptions hurt us, we learn to hide our real selves and stuff our feelings. We end up wearing a mask before God, people, and even ourselves. We slowly but surely become unwilling to even try to know ourselves simply because it seems too frightening and emotional to do so.

Peter Scazzero (whose excellent book *Emotionally Healthy Spirituality* has dramatically impacted my life and deeply influenced this chapter) says it is impossible to be *spiritually* mature while remaining *emotionally* immature. He further states that it is impossible to become emotionally mature without self-knowledge.

Scazzero looks at Jesus' temptation in the wilderness as a case study in the way Satan attacks each of us at our identity. He points out that God handcrafted us, deeply loves us, and accepts us. Knowing that love and delighting in His acceptance of us as we truly are is the only foundation for knowing, loving, and accepting our true selves.

When Satan comes to Jesus as He is fasting in the desert (Matt. 4), Jesus has yet to do a single miracle or die the sacrificial death that would pay the penalty for all humankind's sin. But the Father deeply loves Jesus and already approves of who He is. This is the basis for all of Jesus' personal identity. And yet, Satan comes to convince Him that the Father's love is misplaced and that Jesus is unworthy.

Scazzero identifies the three temptations Satan threw at Christ as the same three areas where he threatens us, making us run from self-knowledge and stunting our relationship with God:

- When Satan came to Christ and tempted Him to prove that He really was the Son of God by turning stones into bread, he was tempting Jesus to believe the lie "I am what I do. My performance is who I am." This is absolutely a temptation in our world today. Too many of us get our self-identity by what we achieve, how useful we are, and what we have accomplished.

- When Satan showed Jesus the magnificence and wealth of the world, he was saying, "Look at what everyone else has. You don't have anything. You're a nobody." The devil was attacking His source of security. He wanted Jesus to believe "I am what I have. My possessions define who I am." This is more twisted thinking in our world today— what we have defines us.

- When Satan invited Jesus to throw Himself down from the highest point of the temple so that people might believe in Him, Jesus was an unknown. Satan wanted Him to believe this lie: "I am what others think I am. My popularity defines me." Most of us are addicted to what others think of us. We are made by the approval of others and destroyed by a single word of criticism.

When we give in to these temptations, we spend our lives in image management, trapped in a self we have created, never knowing who we truly are. Writing an "only God" story with your one and only life—a story that changes you and your world—is an impossibility unless you peel back the layers of pretense, shut down the voices and demands of others, and discern your true value and the vision, calling, and mission the Father has given you.

LEARNING TO UNDERSTAND AND KNOW YOUR TRUE SELF

You can't afford to neglect valuing yourself enough to discover and accept your personality, temperament, likes, dislikes, thoughts, and feelings. Looking into your past to see where you came from and what voices told you what you currently believe is vital to writing a great story. Going there is a fearful thing for most of us, though. But the early church father John Chrysostom encourages us to be brave: "Find the door of your own heart; you will discover it is the kingdom of God."

How can you get started down the road of understanding and knowing your story up to this point in your life? Here are some "action steps" you can begin taking today:

1. Ask God to speak to you through your emotions and memories—then be still and listen. Though most of us don't want others to control our lives, we tend to subconsciously give more credence to the voices of others than to our own inner voice or to the voice of God. Regularly dismiss the "fixing" of others and get alone with God to listen, think, and journal the things He speaks to you. Don't be afraid of silence. This process has been foundational for every giant in the faith.

2. Spend time with people you trust who know themselves and who are in search of a great story. God's healing and hope come through community, not isolation. As you develop transparency and vulnerability, you will become more and more the real you. Invite others to tell you truth; then receive it and process it.

3. Try some new things. For many of us, change feels like death. One counseling axiom says, "The pain of change is so great that a person remains the same until the pain of change becomes less that the pain of things remaining as they are." Never let yourself forget that until you actually discover the authentic you God created you to be, with all the pain of change that requires, you will remain stuck and dying.

4. *Act courageously and persevere, despite what others think.* Not everyone will be happy as they witness you getting healthy enough to write a new story. When you change, they may loudly scream, "Change back!" But don't do it. You have to be brave enough and strong enough to tolerate uncomfortable consequences of growth.

5. *Revisit your past.* Our family heritage, from years and years back, powerfully affects us all. The Bible speaks of curses and blessings traveling for generations in a family line. What happens for good or bad in one generation more often than not repeats itself in the next. Your financial difficulties, sexual sins, marital struggles, emotional baggage—as well as the corresponding good things—most likely have their roots in your family story. As the old proverb states, "The apple doesn't fall far from the tree."

You have to know and understand these chapters before you can write your own story well. Scazzero shows readers how to create a family genogram—a family tree that displays pertinent and shaping information about several generations prior. This was very helpful to me in diagnosing where I currently am, where I come from, and what God wants to do in me. Don't make the mistake of thinking that if you don't think about it, the past isn't real and will go away.

6. *Look at your present strengths and weakness—and at your sinful patterns.* This may be a particularly fearful step for you, but bringing secrets into God's light is the only way to effectively deal with them. Breaking the shame that has held you captive will release you to forgiveness and a shining future.

7. *Proactively seek out all the help you can get.* The current you is the result of all the influences that have been part of your life to this point. You can change your story by bringing new and better influences into your life. First, you need to be in a strong church where the truth is preached every Sunday and where you have the opportunity to process your life and next steps in small, safe, relational groups. Second, seek professional counseling if you need it. We feel no shame in going to the doctor for help with our physical deficiencies, and we should not feel shame in seeking out professional help for our emotional and spiritual difficulties. We are not bodies that happen to have a soul and spirit but primarily spirits and souls housed in bodies. That's why it is even more vital that we get spiritual and emotional help than it is to get physical help. Third, read some good books. God has gifted many wonderful people with the ability to write books that show us how to work with the Spirit of God

to find healing and growth in our deepest areas of need. The Holy Spirit and His great men and women have often been my counselors as I have worked through books that directly addressed my needs. If you are open to seeking help, God will lead you to the right resources as you work on marriage and family issues, obsessions, addictions, brokenness, personality issues, and fears.

8. Rewrite your story according to what God says. Jesus refused Satan's assessments and authored His own story according to the truth His Father had declared about Him. You and I must do the same. God's Word is the truth; Jesus is truth. And Jesus said that knowing and living by the truth sets us free.

KNOWING WHO YOU ARE *IN CHRIST*

God has used Dr. Neil Anderson, founder of Freedom in Christ Ministries, to free me to write an "only God" story. His "Steps to Freedom in Christ" have been a tool for many members on our church team. His resources help a believer take a detailed walk through the past and present and come to a joyful and free acceptance of who he or she is in Christ.

Our position and identity in Christ is the basis for living and growing "in Christ." Sanctification is the consistent, practical outworking of what it means to be a new creation in Christ. John Stott wrote in *God's Good News for the World* that our primary responsibility in the work of sanctification is to constantly remind ourselves of who we are and to remind ourselves to live up to our new identity. In Christ I have been forgiven, have become a child of God, and have willingly become a follower and imitator of Jesus. The power that raised Jesus Christ from the dead is in me. I need to remind myself on a moment-by-moment basis who I now am. . .and *whose* I am.

Knowing who we are in Christ and understanding what it means to be a child of God makes an incredible difference for struggling Christians. It makes *the* difference in whether or not your story is powerful enough to change the world.

Dr. Anderson has compiled scriptures that answer the challenges Satan gave to Jesus more than two thousand years ago. . .and still gives to us today:

I AM ACCEPTED BECAUSE. . .

- I am God's child (John 1:12).
- As a disciple, I am a friend of Jesus Christ (John 15:15).
- I have been justified (Rom. 5:1).
- I am united with the Lord, and I am one with Him in spirit (1 Cor. 6:17).
- I have been bought with a price and I belong to God (1 Cor. 6:19–20).
- I am a member of Christ's body (1 Cor. 12:27).
- I have been chosen by God and adopted as

His child (Eph. 1:3–8).

- I have been redeemed and forgiven of all my sins (Col. 1:13–14).
- I am complete in Christ (Col. 2:9–10).
- I have direct access to the throne of grace through Jesus Christ (Heb. 4:14–16).

I AM SECURE BECAUSE...

- I am free from condemnation (Rom. 8:1–2).
- I am assured that God works for my good in all circumstances (Rom. 8:28).
- I am free from any condemnation brought against me, and I cannot be separated from the love of God (Rom. 8:31–39).
- I have been established, anointed, and sealed by God (2 Cor. 1:21–22).
- I am hidden with Christ in God (Col. 3:1–4).
- I am confident that God will complete the good work He started in me (Phil. 1:6).
- I am a citizen of heaven (Phil. 3:20).
- I have not been given a spirit of fear but of power, love, and a sound mind (2 Tim. 1:7).
- I am born of God, and the evil one cannot touch me (1 John 5:18).

I AM SIGNIFICANT BECAUSE...

- I am a branch of Jesus Christ, the true vine, and a channel of His life (John 15:5).
- I have been chosen and appointed to bear fruit (John 15:16).
- I am God's temple (1 Cor. 3:16).
- I am a minister of reconciliation for God (2 Cor. 5:17–21).
- I am seated with Jesus Christ in the heavenly realm (Eph. 2:6).
- I am God's workmanship (Eph. 2:10).
- I may approach God with freedom and confidence (Eph. 3:12).
- I can do all things through Christ, who strengthens me (Phil. 4:13).

If you read these with a focused heart and mind daily, and if you allow the truth of God to transform your perception of self, you can rewrite the rest of your story. Be fearless. Look your past and present in the face, and discover who you really are. Write a new story as an accepted, secure, and significant child of God.

ACTION STEPS

1. Read *Emotionally Healthy Spirituality*, and then make a personal genogram. Develop a plan for personal growth based on what you learn.

2. Contact Freedom in Christ Ministries (www.ficm.org), and go through the steps to freedom in Christ with a trusted spiritual companion.

3. Make a copy of the "Who I Am in Christ" scriptures, and read them every day.

4

{ Embracing Change }

Riddle: "How many church members does it take to change a lightbulb?"

Answer: "What?? *Change????*"

That joke (insert your chosen denomination in place of the words "church members") has made the rounds of most every church circle, regardless of denominational tradition. The fact that most human beings resist change is widely documented, and an abnormally high percentage of change resisters are within the church of Jesus Christ. That the God of continually morphing and changing creation would have followers whose default mode is critiquing, despising, and condemning change seems oxymoronic.

Because we crave comfort and convenience, we are preconditioned to resist change. But change remains the basis for all hope. Embracing change as an ally for our future is an indispensable ingredient to authoring an amazing story.

The evolutionary biologist Charles Darwin is not a person I frequently quote. However, his study of animal species that endured in the struggle for survival led him to a conclusion I think also applies to success in life: "It is not the strongest of the species that survives, nor the most intelligent, but the one most responsive to change."

I would paraphrase Darwin's words this way: "It is not the strongest person who writes the most amazing story, nor the most intelligent, but the one most responsive to change."

CHANGE: SOMETHING TO BE EMBRACED, NOT FEARED

My life has become incredibly joyful because of change. I stuttered; my speaking changed. I had a crippled leg; my bones grew and healed. I was single; I got married and became part of a beautiful duet. My wife and I had four little babies. That was a wonderful period of life, but how sad and broken we would be today if they had *remained* babies!

Everything wonderful and satisfying in my life has come about because of change. Without a doubt, some changes have been difficult to face and accept, but nothing good would ever have happened in my life without change.

When we understand that change is growth and development, we position ourselves to embrace change. When we realize there can be no progress without change, we are able to see change as a thing of beauty. On the other hand, to not change, to remain in stagnation, is equivalent to death. Nothing can be accomplished by the refusal to move forward.

I was a twenty-four-year-old single man with no prospects of marriage when I was first asked to come to Sugarcreek to pastor a small church. This was a mid-year move, which is very unusual in the church system to which I belonged, but I was just a player in a series of moves necessitated by a moral failure of one of our appointed pastors. Up to that point, my only pastoral experience was a two-year stint as a youth pastor. The church superintendent in Ohio asked me to be a temporary solution for the Sugarcreek Church. I would be appointed for just a few months, until conference time, when a different—make that "married"—pastor could be assigned.

I was willing to embrace change, and the first change God asked me to make was in my willingness to be bold and take risks. My superintendent told me that appointing a young, single man to pastor a church made everyone nervous, because "we had already had ten pastors over the last ten years fall morally." God used that statement to empower and embolden me. I reminded the superintendent that all the men he referenced had been married men.

I felt they were asking the wrong question. The significant question was not, "Is Dwight married or single?" but "Where is Dwight in his walk with God?" If I wasn't right with God, I was in trouble regardless of my marital status. And my age? True, as pastor, I would lead people old enough to be my parents and grandparents. But truth is truth, no matter whose lips speak it. First Timothy 4:12 was like steel in my bones, "Don't let anyone look down on you because you are young, but set an example for the believers in speech, in conduct, in love, in faith and in purity" (NIV).

This was a revolutionary change for me to embrace. I was the youngest child in my family, and I typically deferred, took a backseat, and allowed others to speak for me. But God impressed deep within my spirit that this was a pivotal point of change for me. Whatever happened now would determine the course of my life.

So I held steady. Having no other options, and no one else to fill the spot, the superintendent agreed that if the church hadn't fallen apart by conference business meetings, I would be reappointed and remain as pastor. And here I am, decades later, still writing a story I could never have imagined.

It is providential that God challenged me from the very beginning of my move to the place that has become my lifetime home. I have lived in Sugarcreek now more than double the time I have spent at any other location. Only God knew the way I and everyone around me would need to embrace continual, ongoing, stretching change in order to dream His dreams. This traditional little church in an extremely conservative area, where having a young single pastor was a matter for chitchat in the country shops dotting the town, proved itself to be incredibly gutsy time and again. I set the climate for aggressive and intentional change from the start.

One of the first decisions I made was to ask both the church and myself to embrace musical change. Music is a vital element in setting the culture of a church. The church had an ancient sound system and played it through car speakers. I wasn't sure I could persuade anyone that early in my tenure to invest in change enough to pay for something, so I obtained a personal loan and purchased the first real sound system the church ever owned.

That was a really huge step for me. I have never been a big spender, but I spent my own (well, not my own dollars, but my own credit) money on something I didn't even know I would be permitted to use without a fight. And that wasn't all. The very first Sunday I was in charge of the service, I sang a solo. Yes, you read that correctly. No, singing special music is not in my wheelhouse, and I had never been a soloist. But I had a decent voice, and I knew what kinds of changes we needed to make to attract our culture and potential audience. I had to push through tremendous fear and insecurity to do it. But if I intended to ask the church to embrace hard changes and take new territory, I had to lead the way and do it, too.

SOME HEALTHY PERSPECTIVES ON CHANGE

Though change has been the norm for life on this planet since before God even breathed the breath of life into

Adam, change is difficult for most of us, even under the best of circumstances. Change has not slowed with the passage of time. In fact, in the infancy of the twenty-first century, change seems to come at the speed of light. Though we can't usually slow down change (and I really wouldn't want to), I have adopted several perspectives that give me an edge in adapting well to the changes others initiate—and that give me courage for my own change-related decisions:

Perspective #1—Nothing lasts forever. In his remarkable DVD series, *The Power of Momentum* (with Craig Groeschel), Andy Stanley says that *nothing* has a fifteen- or twenty-year run anymore—in church, in business, or anywhere else. While the sacred covenants we make, such as marriage, are still intended for a lifetime, almost everything else is up for constant change. We frequently move, change jobs and locations, and change brand loyalty. In the past, church and school programs were remarkably the same for the first child in a family as for the last child who came along ten or more years later. Not so today. Textbooks and programs are quickly outdated. More often than not, the best, newest information can be "Googled." Encyclopedias have practically gone out of print due to Internet search engines, a term we didn't even know until well into the nineties. Clearly, nothing lasts the way it is forever, and resisting that fact does not change its reality. When we accept this new reality, we are better equipped for a joyful journey. Embracing impermanence in life prepares us to end the struggle and move forward with anticipation.

Perspective #2—Other perspectives are helpful. Realizing that other people just might know things that can be helpful to you changes your attitude on a deep level. When you see additional perspectives as valuable, when you aren't afraid to look foolish and are willing to ask naive, wide-eyed questions of anyone who is doing anything that matters, you will come to see change as an opportunity to start afresh and win in new ways. You will find yourself listening seriously to thoughts and ideas you might once have dismissed, and the threat related to change will diminish.

Perspective #3—The information "everybody knows" isn't always right. The person who changes his story and changes the world is wary of "common wisdom." First of all, wisdom isn't particularly common, and when a person spends too much energy considering public opinion, he or she will be the person the apostle James describes as "like a wave of the sea, blown and tossed by the wind" (James 1:6 NIV). One day, "everyone" will know that you need a college degree to do anything, and the next day "everyone" will be told just as emphatically that no one is getting a job in that field, degree or no degree, so why bother? The very idea that was rejected a dozen times may just succeed with a slightly different approach or location. In short, "everyone" can be wrong. When you start adjusting your automatic acceptance of "what everyone knows," expect to annoy people—especially the ones who are unhappy with their lives but don't want to change. Arguing rarely helps. It just discourages you and only once in a decade or so makes a convert. I have found my best response to fatalistic prophecies about what "everyone knows" will happen to me if I dare change is a simple, "Hmm. . .really?" I guess I have said "Really?" a couple hundred thousand times over the past twenty-five years.

Perspective #4—Learning to let go is a vital life skill. One of the most challenging realities of life is that not everyone who starts the journey with you will finish it with you. Some people may only like you or want to be with you when you have a certain title, look a certain way, or make the same choices they would make. If you want to change the world, you will have to accept that as okay. You will need to let them be who they are, wish them well, and let them go with love. Positive world changers all develop this skill. One of the most painfully stretching experiences for me is having individuals I love deeply, men who have been in close discipling relationships with me, look intently into my eyes and assure me that if I made a certain change, they would leave the church and end our friendship. It has been most painful to see them make good on their word. But God has helped me let go with love. If I hadn't learned to do that, I could never have the freedom to write the story He is authoring through me today.

Perspective #5—Always look for the good. Change is not always happy. . .or even good. Even though change may come as the result of a negative event, we can choose our response well and find that it leads to something good. There is good in the midst of every change—even the most painful and difficult one. This is a hard concept to absorb initially. As I look back over my experiences, however, I realize that when some "bad" change happened, it always culminated in some type of growth or new thinking that equipped me for a new situation and better place. Romans 8:28 (NASB) teaches that this should not come as a surprise for followers of Jesus Christ: "And we know that God causes all things to work together for good to those who love God, to those who are called according to His purpose."

When you adjust your perspectives, you can begin to embrace the most basic changes, and that will start you on the path to changing your story and your world.

THE COURAGE TO TRY SOMETHING DIFFERENT

Henry Ford was an American industrialist, founder of the Ford Motor Company, and sponsor of the development of the assembly line technique of mass production. His introduction of the Model T automobile revolutionized transportation and industry. His ideas appeared foolish to those who said there would never be a market for the unusual inventions. But he looked at the world as it was, considered how he wanted it to be, and said, "If you always do what you've always done, you'll always get what you've always got."

Taking that a giant leap forward, Christian speakers and preachers have challenged, "If you want God to do something He has never done, He will ask you to do something you have never done." You may have heard both of those statements so many times you can gloss over them without even thinking. But stop right now and highlight those words. Read them aloud:

> *If you always do what you've always done,*
> *you'll always get what you've always got.*
> *If you want God to do something He has*
> *never done, He will ask you to do something*
> *you have never done.*

You know that you have a deep desire to experience something amazing, something supernatural. You want your story to be something that can only be described as "only God." That's why you are reading this book. (Unless you are my dad. Dad's life has already been "only God"! He's reading it because he, quite clearly and without bias, believes I am wonderful—naturally, any book I would write would be fascinating to him!) Your responsibility right now is to begin to create the environment in which God can work.

The first basic change to create your environment is to *change what you really want changed.* Luke 5 records the disciple Peter's life-transforming "only God" moment. This was not Peter's first encounter with Jesus. Sometime earlier, his brother Andrew had heard John the Baptist say with deep conviction, "Behold, the Lamb of God!" Overwhelmed and excited, Andrew immediately went and found Peter and announced, "We have found the Messiah!" Peter ran to meet Jesus for himself.

That began a series of "only God" mini-moments. When Peter met Jesus, his name had been Simon, but Jesus renamed him Peter and characterized him as a rock. Peter was a guest at the wedding where Jesus turned water into wine. On the way to that wedding, Jesus spoke to a fig tree, and the tree did exactly what Jesus said. Jesus led Peter and His followers to Peter's hometown. Peter saw Jesus heal his mother-in-law and witnessed demons being cast out. He heard Jesus teach and saw people respond dramatically.

Powerful "only God" moments!

Yet the Luke 5 account says Peter had returned to his fishing career. How could he have personally witnessed all he saw and still go back to the mundane, ordinary life of a fisherman? Perhaps it was because Peter had observed "only God" moments but had never been an up-close-and-personal player. Peter had lived on the fringes of what God could do. He had seen God work in the lives of others in miraculous, undeniably supernatural ways. But he had never been right at the heart of a personal "only God" story, an experience that could be described in no other way.

Luke tells us about the moment that started the change, the moment that gave Peter the position and power to change the world (vv. 1–11 NIV):

> *One day as Jesus was standing by the Lake of Gennesaret, the people were crowding around him and listening to the word of God. He saw at the water's edge two boats, left there by the fishermen, who were washing their nets. He got into one of the boats, the one belonging to Simon, and asked him to put out a little from shore. Then he sat down and taught the people from the boat.*
>
> *When he had finished speaking, he said to Simon, "Put out into deep water, and let down the nets for a catch."*
>
> *Simon answered, "Master, we've worked hard all night and haven't caught anything. But because you say so, I will let down the nets."*
>
> *When they had done so, they caught such*

*a large number of fish that their nets began
to break. So they signaled their partners
in the other boat to come and help them,
and they came and filled both boats so full
that they began to sink.*

*When Simon Peter saw this, he fell at
Jesus' knees and said, "Go away from me,
Lord; I am a sinful man!" For he and all his
companions were astonished at the catch of
fish they had taken, and so were James and
John, the sons of Zebedee, Simon's partners.*

*Then Jesus said to Simon, "Don't be
afraid; from now on you will fish for people." So they pulled their boats up on shore,
left everything and followed him.*

Peter was one of the very first disciples Jesus personally called, and he chose to follow Him. But Peter's focus
was inconsistent and divided. Sometimes he focused on
Jesus, but sometimes he focused on his own life situation.
Before Jesus called Peter, he was centered on his boats,
his nets, his skills. But in this moment, his focus changed.
When Jesus directly challenged him, Peter turned his attention to Jesus. Peter was a career fisherman, so he knew
well that what Jesus said to do was not the way to do
things. Many objections filled his mind. He was a tired,
worn-out man. He had just spent a long and unfruitful
night on the sea.

But his "only God," life-changing moment took place because *Peter deliberately changed his focus*. He took his eyes off the boat, off the nets. He changed his focus from how weary he was to the fact that Jesus was actually speaking to him.

Peter changed his belief, too. As he sat there in the boat, he knew he had a choice, and a change, to make if there was to be any chance of an "only God" moment. He had to choose to change what he believed.

Peter was an experienced fisherman who had been through years of dry nights and slow days. He knew when the fish were biting and when they weren't. Until this moment, he would never have taken the advice or accepted the direction of a former carpenter, a religious teacher, about fishing.

You know how that is. When a "DINK" (double income, no kids) knowingly informs you what he would do if your cranky, tired son were his kid, you ignore him, discreetly roll your eyes, and, as politely as you have the patience to do so, blow him off. That's what we would have expected Peter to do, too. His belief, right up to that very moment, was that he knew what was best. His experience and training told him what to do. He believed in his experiences and background.

But in that moment, everything changed. Peter changed his belief. He *decided* to change, to go against his feelings, and to say by faith that Jesus knew best. He called Him "Master," a title that recognized Jesus as the ultimate authority. In that significant moment of choice, Peter made a huge leap to alter what he believed. He believed Jesus was God.

That led Peter to another change. If Jesus was his focus, if he truly believed He was God, then Peter needed to change to whom he was listening. This is the moment when Peter's story truly started in a new direction. Before, it was all academic, perfunctory, basically attitudinal changes. Now his *actions* actually changed. Peter answered, "Master, we have worked all day and have caught nothing."

Hear the unspoken message in Peter's words. "Jesus, we are experienced fishermen. We really, truly know how to do this. And we've been working it...we've been doing what we have done our whole adult lives, as our fathers did before us. Today we've been at it since sunup. If we poll all the fishermen in the boats here on the lake, every single one of them will say trying again is foolish—a waste of time. The oldest fishermen to the youngest will all say that this can't possibly work, that this is not the way to do things. And I hate to say it, but I actually agree with them."

But because You say so. . .I will let down the nets.

What a moment! Peter took the leap. He embraced change and went against everything else he had ever heard or been taught. He changed to whom he was listening and chose the command of Jesus above all else. This created the opportunity for an "only God" moment.

If Peter had never obeyed this simple command, he never would have participated in the miracle.

Jesus interrupted Peter's life. Peter sacrificed what was most important about his work—his nets—without knowing what would happen. And let's be honest. There wasn't a ton of risk at this point—just pushing out the boat and lowering the nets. . .again. It wasn't incredibly risky, but it *was* incredibly inconvenient. He was tired and needed his rest. But Peter decided this would be more about Jesus than about him, so he changed his focus, his belief, and to whom he listened. He decided he would take a chance on God's story. He embraced change, and his story would never be the same again.

So now it comes to you and me. If we want an "only God" experience, it starts the same for us. Changing our desires and embracing change is almost always inconvenient. If we aren't willing to embrace the changes, we'll never experience the miracle.

What is it about your focus that needs to change? What has occupied your greatest thoughts and energy up to right now? How about your beliefs? What needs to change in those areas? Is Jesus a "good guy," someone you like to hang with when it's convenient or when you need a miracle. . .or is He *Master*? To whom are you listening? What are the other voices telling you? What would it mean for you to hear and obey the voice of Jesus above all else?

"Only God" stories start right here—in the exact

moment we stop running and resisting. . .and *embrace* change.

ACTION STEPS

1. Which of the five perspectives listed in this chapter poses the biggest challenge for you? Write a prayer expressing your desire to see these areas in a new way. Make a small card with the five perspectives on it, and read it every day.

2. What particular area of your life do you know needs change, yet you resist it? Consciously pray, "Master, show me Your wisdom and perspective about this area of my life." Write down any thoughts that come to you over the next few days. Expect God to give you new insights and help you hear new points of view.

5

{ Enemies of Change }

Here's a thought-provoking question: If becoming a world changer is truly an option for each one of us, why wouldn't everyone embrace the opportunity?

We all are different in our skills, abilities, and personalities. Sadly, though, too many of us share a common self-defeating denominator. When presented with inspiring accounts of others' life changes and equally challenging opportunities to change our own directions, too many of us claim to be uniquely flawed: "I am different," "My church is different," "My family is different," and "My company is different" are some of the mantras that become our excuses for refusing to try a proven approach or adopt a suggested change.

The truth is, though, any one of us can experience the exhilaration of change. That is because we were created for continual growth and forward movement.

The God who conceived of and created every nanogram in the universe is the never-ending source of creativity. Satan is the antithesis of life and newness. He has a limited arsenal, and from the beginning he has used exactly the same techniques to stall new beginnings.

God offered the Israelite slaves in Egypt an open door to freedom and fulfillment in the land of promise, a place beyond anything they had dreamed. Time and again, though, Satan used fear, fatigue, failure, and frustration to derail them. They even spent forty years spinning their wheels in a dead-end desert when the entire trip should have taken less than two weeks. The whole generation, minus two that originally started for the Promised Land, died in the desert. Only Caleb and Joshua defeated their inner enemies and made the necessary changes to author new, exciting chapters in God's story, changing their own lives and legacies.

Every world changer will encounter the same four enemies Caleb and Joshua faced and overcame. If you let them, these adversaries will keep you from a life of significance. On the other hand, if you approach them with faith and courage, as Caleb and Joshua did, God will do what only He can do, and your "only God" story will explode.

Let's take a look at those enemies of change so you can recognize them as they come to do battle with you.

THE ENEMY CALLED FEAR

At its root, fear is a sense of inadequacy or inability to handle a situation or to do or be what is needed. This enemy can take many shapes and forms. Fear can loom large when we believe we lack the experience, the resources, or the support we need to move forward in writing our stories. Fear can be very debilitating and powerful, usually more so than the actual situations we face.

Nicolas Berdyaev was a nineteenth/twentieth-century Russian religious and political philosopher who was fed challenges and fearful situations in daily doses. He reflected, "Fear is never a good counselor, and victory over fear is the first spiritual duty of man."

The very first human illustrates that wisdom.

Adam had a long-standing, intimate relationship with the God who created him. Every day, in the cool of the evening, God walked in the garden with His most-prized creation. But when the serpent questioned the rationale behind God's prohibition of food from just one tree, Adam and his wife, Eve, took counsel of their fear. They allowed the fear that maybe God was hiding something worthwhile from them, that He was withholding an ability they should have, to conquer their former trust. Coached by the fear that they were missing out on something, they disobeyed God.

When God came to the garden that evening to walk, fear was in the captain's chair. Adam and Eve hid from the God who created them and loved them. Adam eventually owned that fear had persuaded them: "We hid because we were afraid." Their first spiritual duty was to overcome fear, but instead they allowed their fears to conquer them. As a result, the story of all humankind took a tragic trajectory.

Whenever change is an option, fear comes calling. We must remember that the counsel fear gives will always be tainted and twisted. It is our duty to gain victory over it.

Eleanor Roosevelt, wife of the thirty-second president of the United States and a woman with a remarkable life story of her own, spoke of defeating fear this way: "You gain strength, courage, and confidence by every experience in which you really stop to look fear in the face. You must do the thing which you think you cannot do."

This is how fear has been and always will be defeated. The apostle Paul wrote to the young pastor Timothy, "For God has not given us a spirit of fear and timidity, but of power, love, and self-discipline" (2 Tim. 1:7 NLT). That niggling feeling that you can and must choose courage and face down fear is God's Spirit in you, giving you the motivation and strength to overcome.

FEAR OF CRITICISM

A few manifestations of fear are particularly common when we consider changing our story. One is the fear of criticism. Most of us have a deep-seated desire to please people, a desire that has served us well in much of our lives. But when we start to make the significant changes God has led us to make, people who are accustomed to the way we have lived so far may object. It's a fearful thing when people we love and respect object to the choices we need to make. More often than not, our fear of their disapproval will shut us down, keeping our story bland and lackluster.

Jesus spoke very clearly about the necessity of rising above the irrational attachment to approval, even from our own families. He said, "If anyone comes to Me, and does not hate his own father and mother and wife and children and brothers and sisters, yes, and even his own life, he cannot be My disciple" (Luke 14:26 NASB).

This "disease to please" can immobilize. Fear of the disapproval from those we count on for provision and praise (such as our mother and father) is daunting. But the psalmist David assures us from his own personal experience, "Even if my father and mother abandon me, the LORD will hold me close" (Ps. 27:10 NLT). I second David's affirmation. When I have faced my fear of criticism and disapproval, even from those I held most dear to my heart, the Lord has come through for me and held me close.

FEAR OF FAILURE

The gigantic fear of failure takes out a lion's share of potential winners—discouraging them from even trying. The word *fail* means "to fall short of success or achievement in something expected, attempted, desired, or approved" (dictionary.com). By this simple definition, we must admit that we all fail.

Since everyone fails, we must proactively decide to take risks. We can anticipate that not everything we try will work, but as we try and sometimes fail, we should seek to learn from our failures rather than allowing the possibility of failure to paralyze us.

The one-talent man in the story Jesus told (Matt. 25:18–29) is a sad example of a man who allowed his fear of failure to keep him from a blessing. He was afraid to try, so he hid his talent in the ground, expecting his master to accept his excuses. That exact fear is the reason many people fail. Some won't try at all, and some try only halfheartedly because of their fear. They think, *If I don't try, I won't fail; therefore, I'll succeed.*

When we allow fear to paralyze us, we guarantee failure. William Shakespeare said, "Our doubts are traitors, and make us lose the good we oft might win, by fearing to attempt." You might just succeed beyond anything you can imagine—if you face your fear and actually try.

FEAR OF. . .SUCCESS?

Ironically, discussion of the fear of failure leads us to its cousin—the fear of success. But who would be afraid of success? The author of this book, for one.

For a long time, I didn't realize how this giant held me back. Actually, this fear has held many members of my family hostage. I think his footprints are often clearly discernible in families in which humility is highly valued. The side effects of success ("People may think I think I am somebody," "I may have to change my associations," "People may expect more of me," "Success will make me a bigger target for criticism," "It's going to be so much pressure to maintain success after I get there, it would be better to just stay here," etc.) are really what prompt this kind of fear.

Unlike fear of failure, fear of success is almost always unconscious and therefore far more insidious. Because this fear is generally subconscious, we can easily avoid confronting and overcoming it. Fears we never consciously acknowledge have a tendency to grow stronger. And as time goes by, it becomes harder and harder to take action.

Think about it. What might happen if you succeed? If you lose the weight. . .get the job. . .earn the money. . . start the business. . .get pregnant. . .get the degree. . .quit smoking. . .adopt the child. . .write the book. . .stretch yourself? What stops you from moving forward?

A statement often misattributed to Nelson Mandela but actually written by activist/author Marianne Williamson strikes a chord so deeply that it has been quoted in numerous speeches and even movies—from *Akeelah and the Bee* to *Coach Carter*. Here is what Williamson said: "Our deepest fear is not that we are inadequate. Our deepest fear is that we are powerful beyond measure. It is our light, not our darkness, that most frightens us. We ask ourselves, who am I to be brilliant, gorgeous, talented, and fabulous?"

Ms. Williamson challenges self-defeating thoughts and challenges us to ask, who are we *not* to be brilliant, gorgeous, talented, and fabulous? We are actually children of almighty God.

I agree completely. There is nothing helpful to me or to others about me shrinking back, feeling inadequate, minimizing myself, and playing small. I am called to be the light of the world, and I cannot do that when I shrink and hide and make sure no one thinks I think I am somebody.

When I step up to the plate and be all I can be, I open the door of possibility for others to believe in themselves as well. People will take their cues from me. If I succeed, I make it even more likely that they will, too.

THE FEAR OF RESPONSIBILITY

I have to admit, the fear of responsibility often dogs me. At times I have wanted to run from responsibility. Many days, I have desperately wanted to resign from the church. Taking action, leading others to change, and taking responsibility—these invite scrutiny and vulnerability, and I didn't want anyone looking at me that way. Sometimes, I've wanted the buck to stop somewhere else.

Our culture has practically made an Olympic sport of the refusal to take responsibility for behavior and decisions. That is because anyone who takes responsibility also accepts a level of vulnerability, and that is very uncomfortable for most of us. We dream of how things should and could be if we act, but the particular fear can stop us at the gate.

When the Emancipation Proclamation took effect in the Unites States in 1863, some of the slaves who had been granted their freedom chose to remain in slavery simply because the responsibilities associated with freedom frightened them too much. They found some comfort in their slavery. As slaves, at least they knew what would happen next.

We all want the freedom that taking personal responsibility gives us, but too many of us fear responsibility itself. Consequently, we often opt for the status quo—no responsibility—and lose out on writing a great personal story.

THE ENEMY CALLED FAILURE

You may not like hearing this, but there is an excellent chance that you will have to endure significant failure at some time in your life.

That's true for all of us. Not everything we do will yield the results we desire—certainly not in the time frame we desire them. When we hit that wall of disappointment, our first thought is almost always to cry "uncle!" and throw in the towel. But at the root of this all-too-human response to failure is a very flawed perspective, namely that we tend to associate our identity with our track record. The way we see it, success proves that we are more valuable, while failure proves we aren't worth much. God assures us in His written Word that this is faulty thinking. Colossians 2:10 (NKJV) tells us, "You are complete in him." I don't have to have an unbroken record of success to be adequate or complete in Christ. I already *am* that, regardless of my successes or failures.

Jesus Christ Himself was the perfect example of this principle of completeness. Before He did a single miracle, His Father in heaven affirmed Him and announced that Jesus was His much-loved Son (see Matt. 3:13–17).

Our identity is not dependent on an unbroken string of successes but on the fact that we are complete in the One who was a success in every way. We have a Father in heaven who is pleased with us and calls us His beloved children.

I have also learned that failure is simply an event and not what defines me. I have gone through a string of failures, some that seemed epic at the time, but they have not derailed my story. God has helped me see past failures and say from my heart, "My concern is making sure I obey God the best I can, no matter the outcome."

If you are going to change your story and change the world, you have to see your inevitable failures in a new way. Speaker and author Denis Waitley says, "Failure is just the fertilizer for success." I know that has proved true in my life. I know that every instance of failure in my life has been an opportunity to see and experience God in a way I have never seen or experienced Him before.

Thomas Edison was a good example of someone who learned from his failures and eventually achieved world-changing success. Edison tried more than one thousand combinations of gas and filament before he found a lightbulb that would last. After the lightbulb became a popular public commodity, the science editor of a national publication asked Edison how it felt to have failed so many times. Edison was dumbstruck at the question. He responded that he didn't see his work as a series of failures, but that he had actually eventually succeeded in producing the incandescent bulb. When the interviewer persisted in following this line of questioning, Edison described making the lightbulb as a journey with over one thousand steps along the way. He said, "I failed my way to success!"

George Bernard Shaw said, "A life spent making mistakes is not only more honorable, but more useful than a life spent doing nothing." Failure is a given in life, but it's not final unless you allow it to be. Don't let an instance of failure—or a string of failures—kill your inspiration and ability to pick up the pen and keep writing.

OUR THIRD ENEMY: FATIGUE

General George Patton, best known for his gruff and effective leadership in World War II, and Vince Lombardi, best known for coaching the Green Bay Packers to several championships in the 1960s, are both quoted as saying, "Fatigue makes cowards of us all."

Indeed, fatigue slowly creeps in for the kill when we are physically drained, when we have been battling exceptionally hard or long, when we have seen few victories, and even, surprisingly, right after a major win. It tatters our nerves, encourages physical illness, and impairs our judgment.

The Bible has much to say about the importance of not becoming overly fatigued. You can find one example of this in the Gospel of Mark. Jesus' reputation for teaching, touching, and healing preceded Him to every village, and that made for a very busy, very draining schedule. Despite the relentless pace and seemingly unending line of people who needed help, Jesus made rest for Himself and for the disciples who assisted Him a priority: "Then, because so many people were coming and going that they did not even have a chance to eat, he said to them, 'Come with me by yourselves to a quiet place and get some rest'" (Mark 6:31 NIV).

Second Corinthians 1 records the apostle Paul's admission of pressure and fatigue. He wrote that he had been fighting the battle so long and so hard that he felt as if he had received a sentence of death.

In the midst of one of our first building phases, I felt that sentence myself. We had to renovate our parking lot, and the sloping terrain presented quite a few challenges. I handed the job off and said to myself, *Someone else can do this now. I am too tired.* We were in the middle of a lawsuit regarding shoddy work done on the building construction, and few things about the project had gone as expected. After dealing with that for so long, I just didn't feel I could take on the parking lot, too. But there were so many challenges to getting it done that it kept coming back to my desk.

A very competent, trusted friend took over the parking lot project on the condition he would answer only to me, not a committee, and that he would have the liberty to do it correctly. The original bid to fix the lot was $10,000, but once the project started, the gravel alone ended up costing that much. We had to bring in three hundred semi-truckloads of dirt just to terrace it properly. Watching through my office window as truckload after truckload arrived, I literally worried myself sick over how this would affect my reputation as a leader—and looked for someone to blame. (That's another of the negative side effects of fatigue—failure to take responsibility.) I couldn't stay in my office.

I got in my aging white Honda and took off on an escape run. Around noon, I turned on my favorite Christian radio station, and a speaker's words pierced through my fog: "You may feel that a team of horses is racing toward you, but God has hold of the reins. He is not out to destroy you, but to build your faith." I hit a bump in the road and my defective radio lost the station, but that sound bite—a direct message from God—gave me the courage to go on that day.

The next day, I visited a friend in a hospital about an

hour away, just to get out of town and not have to stare out the office window at my problem. I was so weary and discouraged. Again, at noon God spoke to me through the radio. This time it was Charles Stanley's velvety voice preaching from Mark 11: "Have faith in God. If you say to this mountain. . . What are you saying to your mountain? What have you been saying? Where have you been telling God that He can't and won't work? Some of you listening to me right now need to repent because you have placed more faith in Satan to destroy you than in God to develop you" (my paraphrase).

God had me. Right there in the car, I repented. "God, I am so sorry. I have told You in every possible way that this will destroy me instead of build me. But I am done. If it means I have to pay on this parking lot for the next twenty-five years, Satan has had enough fun with me. I refuse to doubt and worry and wear myself out any longer."

The next day I was back in my office, with a new attitude and a new resolve. That very day, a precious senior saint stopped by. Anna Hershberger, a founding member of the church, had prayed, sacrificed, and believed God to do something great in this community for nearly fifty years before this young, inexperienced preacher arrived. She had spent hours every day in prayer, listening to God, claiming "mountains" by faith, and interceding on behalf of her church, her pastor, her family, and her friends.

After walking with me among the huge piles of dirt

to get into the church, Anna inquired, "Pastor, how are you doing?"

"Well, Anna, we're trying to get this done."

"Pastor, I only ask one thing," she said. "Whatever it costs, do it right. I don't want my car door closing on my leg because the slope of the ground doesn't get fixed."

Before Anna left, she gave me a check big enough to finish up the job. A day or two later, the company hauling our stone gave us a 10 percent discount, too. Wow!

Paul continued in 2 Corinthians with his postbattle perspective:

> *We do not want you to be uninformed, brothers and sisters, about the troubles we experienced in the province of Asia. We were under great pressure, far beyond our ability to endure, so that we despaired of life itself. Indeed, we felt we had received the sentence of death. But this happened that we might not rely on ourselves but on God, who raises the dead. He has delivered us from such a deadly peril, and he will deliver us again. On him we have set our hope that he will continue to deliver us, as you help us by your prayers. Then many will give thanks on our behalf for the gracious favor granted us in answer to the prayers of many.*
> 2 CORINTHIANS 1:8–11 NIV

In the middle of the battle, fatigue can be so overwhelming that we may feel like quitting on something God is preparing to bless. So never underestimate the power of physical, emotional, and spiritual care and renewal.

Change takes energy. We are in a fight for ideas, for resources, and *against* temptation. When we are tired, we can more easily be tempted to quit. We convince ourselves that, once we are not so tired, we can handle the consequences of quitting. Fatigued, we believe a lie, and we make a permanent decision based on a temporary situation.

One of the ways God planned for us to have enough energy supply for the adventures He plans for us is the Sabbath. God built the Sabbath for our rest, and promises particular blessings if we honor it:

> *"If you keep your feet from breaking the Sabbath and from doing as you please on my holy day, if you call the Sabbath a delight and the LORD's holy day honorable, and if you honor it by not going your own way and not doing as you please or speaking idle words, then you will find your joy in the LORD, and I will cause you to ride in triumph on the heights of the land and to feast on the inheritance of your father Jacob." For the mouth of the LORD has spoken.*
> ISAIAH 58:13–14 NIV

In times of particular stress and busyness, Satan has often slyly suggested that I am too busy for a Sabbath. So I begin to push through my weeks and not take my time off. Then God reminds me, "Dwight—you are careful to obey and trust Me with your money, but you won't trust Me with your time. Don't you remember that I can do more in five days than you can do in seven?"

Are you truly authoring an "only God" story? If so, all His principles matter. You defeat fatigue by trusting Him and doing as He says. As the prophet Isaiah wrote, "He gives power to the weak, and to those who have no might He increases strength. Even the youths shall faint and be weary, and the young men shall utterly fall, but those who wait on the LORD shall renew their strength; they shall mount up with wings like eagles, they shall run and not be weary, they shall walk and not faint" (Isa. 40:29–31 NKJV).

THE FOURTH ENEMY: FRUSTRATION

Leon Trotsky, the leader of Russia's October 1917 revolution, once said, "Life is not an easy matter. . . . You cannot live through it without falling into frustration and cynicism unless you have before you a great idea which raises you above personal misery, above weakness, above all kinds of perfidy and baseness."

But even when you have the great idea, you can become well acquainted with frustration, because things rarely work exactly the way we want them to the first time through.

An eighteen-month-old child *knows* how to open a bottle. He's seen his mother and father do it thousands of times, and he knows precisely how it is supposed to happen. But his motor skills are not there yet. He will mess with the bottle, imitating what he has seen until his frustration peaks. Then, he'll either throw down the bottle in frustrated rage or break down wailing in disappointment.

Most of us have a bit better composure than a toddler, but the end results are the same when we become frustrated or discouraged: a dead stall.

Galatians 6:9 (NLT) urges us to move beyond frustration and discouragement: "So let's not get tired of doing what is good. At just the right time we will reap a harvest of blessing if we don't give up." One application of this verse goes like this: Pulling back for a moment, getting a fresh perspective and renewed energy may allow us to see that the harvest of blessing is the very next chapter in our new stories.

We have enemies who vigorously oppose our efforts to change ourselves and the world. Fear, failure, fatigue, and frustration are four of my most familiar foes. But whatever opposition we face, we have this assurance:

> *What, then, shall we say in response to*
> *these things? If God is for us, who can be*
> *against us? He who did not spare his own*
> *Son, but gave him up for us all—how will*

he not also, along with him, graciously give us all things? Who will bring any charge against those whom God has chosen? It is God who justifies. Who then is the one who condemns? No one. Christ Jesus who died— more than that, who was raised to life—is at the right hand of God and is also interceding for us. Who shall separate us from the love of Christ? Shall trouble or hardship or persecution or famine or nakedness or danger or sword? As it is written:

"For your sake we face death all day long; we are considered as sheep to be slaughtered."

No, in all these things we are more than conquerors through him who loved us. For I am convinced that neither death nor life, neither angels nor demons, neither the present nor the future, nor any powers, neither height nor depth, nor anything else in all creation, will be able to separate us from the love of God that is in Christ Jesus our Lord. ROMANS 8:31–39 NIV

ACTION STEPS

1. Wherever you are on your journey, what enemy threatens your next step? Fear? Failure? Fatigue? Frustration? Write an honest letter to God about what you are feeling.

2. Ask God to calm your spirit and direct your steps. Look up scriptures that specifically address your enemy and memorize them. Quote them daily as you gain the strength to move forward in obedience.

6

{ Elements of a Great Story }

All the great stories of humankind have similar elements: setting, plot, characters, conflict, and theme. In chapter 2, we took a quick look at God's amazing story of redemption, and how all of those story pieces fit together to spin the story of His plan for salvation.

Figuring out what these elements are in your life story and sorting out what needs to be rewritten is another vital step in creating your best story. When you do that, you can write a much bigger adventure than you ever thought possible.

In this chapter, you will learn how you can identify the elements of your own story, what you need to change, and how you can make those changes. Let's start with your story's setting.

YOUR STORY'S SETTING

Where is the action (or the boredom) taking place? Did you know that where you are and when you are is not an accident, a random happenstance? J. B. Phillips para-phrased Paul's speech to the Athenians this way:

> *"From one forefather he has created every*
> *race of men to live over the face of the whole*
> *earth. He has determined the times of their*
> *existence and the limits of their habitation,*
> *so that they might search for God, in the*
> *hope that they might feel for him and find*
> *him—yes, even though he is not far from*
> *any one of us."*
> Acts 17:26–27

Your nationality and the space on the timeline of history you occupy is God's gift to you. He has uniquely built into the setting of your story opportunities just for you to find Him and His amazing purpose for your life. As Ephesians 1:11 says, "It's in Christ that we find out who we are and what we are living for" (MSG).

When you embrace the facts of your birth (your nationality, race, and parenthood) and begin to celebrate the time frame God has given you to write your story, you are free to make adjustments and changes within that setting to make yours the best story possible.

Perhaps God has planted an idea for a change in location. Not long ago, I heard of a married couple who had recently turned fifty. Empty nesters, they felt God's prompting to change the setting of their story. They left secure jobs to take the risks of developing a ministry to urban poor in the heart of one of our nation's largest cities.

Maybe you are sensing a pull to a new career, an untried workplace, a different ministry, or an educational pursuit. God did not give you your one and only life to spend it in a monotonous repetition of meaningless and unfulfilling activity. He built you for greatness and contribution. Jesus said He came in order that we might have true life, full, and overflowing (see John 10:10). Maybe a change in your setting is a choice to consider as you pursue that full and overflowing life.

Perhaps a change in your actual physical setting is not necessary. Maybe what you need to change about the setting of your story is how you relate to it. In *Necessary Endings*, a must-read book for story changers, author Henry Cloud says it is not necessary to respond to every negative situation with big—and sometimes heartbreaking—moves like a divorce, a move, or a dissolution. This book teaches that we need to adopt new rules or change our attitudes about some of the settings we are in.

I came within inches of blowing it in this area early in my leadership. We were maxing out our single Sunday service in our first building, attendance-wise. With confidence, I presented my plan for going to two services, thus doubling our outreach and dealing with our overcrowding problem. To my amazement and frustration, the board defeated my proposal. They voted it down. The way I saw it, they voted *me* down.

I was done. I told my wife, "These people do not want to grow, and I'm not wasting my time here anymore. I am resigning. This will no longer be my people or my church."

God gave me some doctoral-level instruction over the next few days. He clearly informed me that these were never "my people" and this was never "my church." It *all* belonged to Him. He also filled me in on the fact that He would clearly let me know when it was time for me to leave Sugarcreek and that He would not deliver this message through my anger. I am so glad I changed the way I dealt with my setting and that I stayed put in this wonderful place where God has grown me and used me.

Instead of worrying and fretting, instead of trying to write parts of your story on your own, take the time to talk with God about your setting. Quit wishing you were younger/older/in a different family. Look for one-of-a-kind opportunities right where you are. Ask God what you can do to magnify everything He has given you. Even if you think your life setting is weak or undesirable and there's nothing you can do to significantly upgrade it, remember the counterintuitive methods our amazing God uses: "But God chose the foolish things of the world to shame the wise; God chose the weak things of the world to shame the strong" (1 Cor. 1:27 NIV) and "He [God] said, 'My grace is all you need. My power works best in weakness.' So now I am glad to boast about my weaknesses, so that the power of Christ can work through me" (2 Cor. 12:9 NLT).

YOUR STORY'S PLOT

In the 1640s, English and Scottish religious scholars wrote *The Westminster Shorter Catechism*, a document intended to educate laypersons in matters of life and faith. Many theologians consider it one of the great documents of our faith. It is written in a question-and-answer format, and the very first Q&A is:

> Q. 1. What is the chief end of man?
> A. Man's chief end is to glorify God (Ps. 86, Isa. 60:21, Rom. 11:36, 1 Cor. 6:20 and 10:31, Rev. 4:11) and to enjoy Him forever (Ps. 16:5–11, Isa. 12:2, Luke 2:10, Phil. 4:4).
> *(Scripture references added by the author)*

The plot of any story is the sequence of events and how they relate to each other. As *The Westminster Shorter Catechism* states, the overall plot of the story of humankind is to glorify God and enjoy life with Him, now and forever.

That should be the chief determining factor when we are deciding whether or not a new direction is right for us. Does this new direction bring glory to God and enhance my relationship with Him? This is vital because

God is a God of glory. The glory of God/bringing glory to God is a mega-theme in the Bible, appearing about 275 times in the English translations, fifty times in the book of Psalms alone.

When you make decisions about your day-to-day activity, when you find yourself in friendships and facing opportunities and working relationships with people who disagree with you and pressure you to turn another direction, the one question you have to ask yourself is, "Will this glorify God?"

But what if you truly don't know whether or not a particular choice glorifies God? Our culture certainly won't give you many clues on choices that glorify God. Whenever you don't know the answer to that all-important question, look to Jesus, whose words and actions show us how to glorify God. Here are a few life-choice scenarios—some you may face yourself—and how Jesus would have handled them:

- *I have been mistreated and am justifiably angry. I'd like to give them a piece of what they gave me.* Revenge and retaliation don't glorify God. Jesus was criticized, betrayed, insulted, and persecuted, but He never retaliated or took revenge. He was strong and manly but never motivated by personal anger. Patience and forgiveness toward those who wrong you glorifies God.

- *I am in love and really tempted. Is it okay for me to have sex if I'm not married?* Sex outside of marriage does not glorify God. Jesus was a single man who lived to be thirty-three, well past the normal age of marriage, and He remained sexually pure all the way. Purity glorifies God.

- *If I tell the exact truth, I may lose my job. I need to protect my future.* Jesus *was* truth, and He never lied or manipulated facts to His advantage. Honor and honesty glorify God.

- *I like to drink a little. What's the big deal if I get drunk occasionally?* Jesus managed His desires and never lost control or needed anything outside His relationship with the Father to empower Him. Self-control glorifies God.

Jesus had many opportunities to be dishonest, manipulative, angry, lazy. He felt every emotion we feel, and yet He never sinned but always brought glory to His Father. He lived intentionally to do that.

John 17 is the record of Jesus' conversation with His Father the night before He was crucified. He confidently reported, "I have glorified you on earth by completing the work you sent me to do" (vs. 4).

Jesus lived intentionally to glorify God, so He was able to confidently pray that short summary of his life. You can live with that same intentionality and confidence. When you consider your plotline, never move away from what brings glory to God. Judge every decision by that principle, and He will make sure you enjoy Him forever.

One more thing: Never underestimate the implications of an apparently small change in your plotline. Think for a moment. If you could change one event in your story up to this point, what would it be? Some of us would have asked that girl to the prom. Some of us wouldn't have asked the girl we did. Some of us wouldn't have chosen to go to that school. Some of us would. . . Well, you get the idea.

I have come to realize that there truly are no "small" moments or "small" decisions. Even what may seem like the most insignificant decisions we make affect our entire lives—for good or for bad. Each moment of your life affects the next, and the next, and so on. Each choice we have made, every moment we have lived, is a part of a chain of events that ultimately made us who we are and directed our life story to this point.

Sliding Doors is a 1998 movie starring Gwyneth Paltrow, who plays Helen, a young public relations worker who has just been fired from her job. The movie begins with Helen racing to catch the tube train, and from that point the movie tells two parallel stories. In one story, Helen makes the train and gets home just in time to catch her boyfriend cheating on her. In the other story, she misses the train and never discovers his infidelity. As the plotline progresses, the woman grows into two totally different people based on the ripple effects of that one apparently minor event.

That's not just simple fiction. Our life stories are often altered in major ways by a choice or event we were positive was inconsequential—if we even stopped to think about it. So pay close attention to the words of the apostle Paul, the author of an amazing life story: "So whether you eat or drink or whatever you do, do it all for the glory of God" (1 Cor. 10:31 NIV).

THE CHARACTERS IN YOUR STORY

The characters in your story are the ones taking action, the ones making the choices, the ones around whom the plot revolves. Of course, if you are a believer, Jesus is the central character in your story.

Or is He?

The man known for centuries as "the rich young ruler" (see Mark 10:17–27) obviously believed in Jesus. He believed Jesus had the key to eternal life. But something in his life took priority over Jesus. He never put Jesus at the center of his life, and the last we know, he was writing sorrow into his story line.

Sadly, many professing Christians do the same thing. Sure, we say we "know" Jesus, and we may even demonstrate some of the attitudes and actions of a true follower of Christ. But we haven't truly made Him the lead character in our stories.

Having Jesus at the center of your story requires you to adopt a specific attitude, one that says: "If Jesus wants it for me, I will not be satisfied without it. If Jesus doesn't want it for me, I don't want it—no way, no how."

Jesus as the central character helps you make the best possible choices concerning the other players in your life story. I remember many years ago hearing John Maxwell say, "Where you are ten years from now will be determined by the books you read and the people with whom you associate." Now, several decades later, I completely affirm the truth of those words.

First, about the books you read. . . Books are like friends. The authors are people who shape you. They actually become influential supporting characters in your story. Over the years, I have read everything Andy Stanley has written, all of Charles Swindoll's books, and all of Neil Anderson's works. I have read the writings of Dallas Willard, J. I. Packer, Jerry Bridges, Dan DeHaan, Elisabeth Elliot, Paul Tournier, Charles Stanley, Billy Graham, Richard Foster, and Craig Groeschel. I have read John the apostle, John Bunyan, John Ortberg, John Piper, and everything John Maxwell has written. I am a voracious reader, and these people and so many others (only a few of whom I have ever actually met) have led me to laugh, cry, ponder, repent, choose, and create.

I have also invited the best characters into my story

by attending conferences and hearing speakers. At just the right times, God has used Rick Warren, Bill Hybels, T. D. Jakes, Jim Collins, Brenda Salter McNeil, and a host of others to speak truth into my life, influence me toward a big story, and keep me from choosing mediocrity. I'm always listening to something from the most challenging teachers to inspire, motivate, and instruct me along the way.

My parents were deliberate in planning and preparing to bring wonderful people into the lives of their children. They knew such people would stretch us and enable us to dream the stuff great lives are made of. Dad and Mom made sure we had access to every missionary and hero in the faith who came through our area, so missionaries like World War II hero Jacob DeShazer became family to us. DeShazer was a bombardier on the historic mission April 18, 1942, in which Gen. Jimmy Doolittle and his crew attacked Tokyo and turned the tide of the Pacific War. For the next three years, Jake paid a heavy price for his bravery as the Japanese beat, tortured, and starved him as a "war criminal." He returned to Japan after the war and served his life in missionary service there. One of the thousands of Japanese who came to faith because of the love Jake and his wife Florence consistently demonstrated was Mitsuo Fuchida, the man who led the raid on Pearl Harbor. DeShazer and Fuchida toured the island in crusades together. These great people and their stories birthed in me a love of ministry and a heart for the world.

I became acquainted with John Maxwell when I was an elementary school boy, and he was in a college quartet that came to our church at least once a year. Just watching how he handled himself and knowing how he lived his life inspired me to plan a little bigger.

As I became a young adult and started making my own choices about the central characters in my life, my future brother-in-law, Charles Young, became an early key player. He dated my sister all through college and invested considerable time in developing a relationship with me through our mutual love of sports. We became like true brothers. As I graduated from college, Charlie gave me the opportunity to partner with him in his aggressive pastoring, which was a whole new style in our denominational setting. More size to my dreams. I was serving as youth pastor in the church where Charlie was lead pastor when I caught the attention of Ohio leadership enough to get a chance to serve in Sugarcreek. In our area of Ohio, most everyone knows The Chapel and the former pastor Knute Larson. I asked Pastor Larson to mentor me and my church. The story grew. Bobb Biehl talked straight and direct to me for two days, one day about the church and one day about me personally. Upsized again. Bruce Smith of Church Solutions Group recently did some consulting for me and for NewPointe. Some of his guidance was hard to hear, but again, changing the story in constructive and challenging ways grew us, not just numerically, but in our impact on the world.

It's a long and inspiring list—the many people who have added color and substance to my life story. Some of them came into my story line by marvelous serendipity, but most of them I intentionally pursued. The list continues to grow even now. Successful businessmen within my own church and community are always on my radar. I make a practice of seeking them out and taking them to lunch or breakfast to ask questions and gain their wisdom. I have driven three to four hours many times to have a sixty-minute lunch with a pastor I didn't yet personally know but knew was ahead of me in leadership.

I can tell you from experience that purposely adding great characters to your own story is worth whatever effort it takes.

Friends are primary contributors to your life story. God has blessed me with friends who support and challenge and grow me, but from time to time, I have had to let some friendships leave the story line. "Necessary endings" as Dr. Henry Cloud put it. Sometimes a friend's values and perspectives will differ so greatly from your own that continuing that friendship will hijack your story and take it in a completely different direction from the one obedience calls you to go. At the very least, that friend's editing will diminish your story. You have to surround yourself with big characters to write a big story. If you are going to have an honorable story, you need to add characters of integrity.

One role that has perhaps more to do with the size of your story than any other is the one your spouse plays. In college, I fell deeply in love with a young woman without considering the impact she would have on the story I could write. Obeying God by ending our engagement was harder than I could have imagined. I couldn't fathom that I would ever again find another person so beautiful who would love me, and I was sure I was destined to write alone. After taking a few years to allow God to grow me and show me that *He* was enough, He allowed me to take a second look at a college classmate I was not mature enough to consider before. God very quickly showed me the adventure that could be mutually ours.

I know it's gentlemanly to say I married above myself, but that was no longer true by the time I married Patty Carson. God had grown both of us to the point that our values and commitments were a solid match, and we committed ourselves to a lifetime of coauthoring the biggest story we could write together.

A little footnote as you consider characters for your story: Don't be afraid when God prompts you to add someone to your story line who will call you out to a greater sacrifice than you had planned. This person might not be one you had thought of for a lead role.

When your response is right, characters He brings to you will enrich your life, even if you don't initially see how.

TIME FOR SOME CONFLICT

Conflict is an element you don't have to plan or write into your story. It will arise whether or not you want it. Conflict in a story line is the struggle the central characters have with opposing forces. What the struggle is and what your obstacles are—these are not really the significant issues. What *is* significant is how you choose to face the conflict.

Conflict in your story *will change on a regular basis*. Sometimes it will be relational, other times emotional, physical, financial, or spiritual. But the tension conflict always brings helps you discover what you stand for. Conflict, if you take it on appropriately, moves your life story forward, and it will be a great story as long as you keep your purpose and goal in mind.

Remember the assurance of your Father in Jeremiah 29:11 (NIV). This word came first to His people when they were in the midst of great conflict and struggle as captives in a foreign land: " 'For I know the plans I have for you,' declares the LORD, 'plans to prosper you and not to harm you, plans to give you hope and a future.' "

That plan and promise is true for you, too.

WRITING YOUR THEME

The theme is the central idea or thought of the story. It can be summed up in a sentence. Here are some examples:

- "A strong-willed Southern belle with a deep love of the land survives the Civil War and determines to rebuild her home." Right. You know that is Margaret Mitchell's *Gone with the Wind*.

- "An insidious villain destroys the homes of two brothers and, while pursuing the third, is outwitted and boiled alive." Ouch! You recognize that as a stripped-down and harsh summary of *The Three Little Pigs*.

- "A rebellious and reckless son leaves home to squander his father's riches but is forgiven and restored when he humbly returns home." You've got it. That's "The Prodigal Son," as told by Jesus.

In his book *Drive*, Daniel Pink tells the story of life-changing advice given to a U.S. president. Clare Booth Luce of Connecticut was one of the first women to serve in the United States Congress. She was later an adviser to President John F. Kennedy. One day she told him, "A great man is one sentence. What's your sentence?" She told him that Abraham Lincoln's sentence was, "He preserved the Union and freed the slaves" and that Franklin Roosevelt's was, "He lifted us out of a Great Depression and helped us win a world war."

Luce was quite concerned that Kennedy's attention was so split in different directions that his "sentence" would be a "muddled paragraph."

You don't have to be president of the United States to understand and benefit from that advice. Investing time in thinking about your sentence is a powerful tool for orienting your life toward a greater story and purpose. You can't do everything, but you can choose something great. Your life story is your greatest legacy. How would you want to sum it up? Figuring out the theme of your life is the way to write a story you'll be proud to have told.

Most often, what holds people back from greatness is not lack of ambition but lack of direction. Figuring out your sentence will give you direction for filling in the details of your story. Without a succinct idea of your theme—a picture of a desired end—the story falls apart along the way.

I want my sentence to read like this: "Dwight Mason focused on eternity, trusted God completely, and followed Him fearlessly, relentlessly, and obediently to change the world." You know, it gives me a rush just to say that. Most days, I can't wait to get out of bed because I know God is pleased with my purpose. He gave it to me, so He is more committed than even I am to bringing it to fulfillment. I live in the anticipation that my next phone call, the next conversation, the next person I meet could be the key to a miracle chapter my world needs.

Remember, it's not only how the stories end that is important but what the main character becomes on the way to the end. After Jesus, you are the main character in your story. Write yourself big. Keep on growing until the story is over.

ACTION STEPS

1. Take a moment to ask yourself about the story you are living right now. Is this the best story for you?

2. Spend a few days thinking about your sentence. Write it and memorize it.

3. What changes do you need to make in your story line in order for your sentence to come true?

4. What kinds of characters do you need to add or subtract from your story in order for God to give you the best success?

7

{ Sharing Your Story }

Many in the group were wiping tears as the man on the platform finished speaking. Applause filled the room, and my friend leaned over to me and whispered, "I'm grateful for my Christian upbringing, but. . ." His voice trailed off. ". . .I certainly don't have a jaw-dropping story to share. I actually don't have much of a testimony." He was expressing the thoughts that hinder many believers from making the "only God" impact they are intended to have with their one and only lives.

People frequently tell me they don't believe they have a story to tell. Actually, that's impossible. The Bible teaches that your life is a letter for the world to read (see 2 Cor. 2:3–5).

Others tell me they just *couldn't* share their story—that they don't know how or are too reserved to do so. Fact is, you *are* sharing your story. It's not that you *have* a testimony; you *are* a testimony. It's not that you *have* a story; you *are* a story. The question is, how can you make opportunities to share your story in a proactive, positive way?

Sharing your story is more than speaking—it's inviting others into your life. It is giving them the opportunity to be a part of the world-changing adventure with you. Part of the excitement of living an adventure is initiating creative opportunities to tell and show others about the life that is available to them, the life they perhaps haven't even dreamed.

STORYBOARDING YOUR OWN STORY

Let's think about your story. Perhaps you have never before considered just how much you have to share. Here's a good way to get started. Make a page with five columns like this:

Successes Troubles Opportunities Relationships Yearnings

Then, down the side of the page, divide your life into stages, up to your current age, like this:

Birth–5

Grade School

High School

**Young
Adult**

Midlife

**Senior
Years**

Once you've finished the chart, take a week or two
to pray and ask God to help you remember the events
in your life that fit into those categories and how He has
used them to teach you, grow you, draw you to Himself,
and make a difference. As the events come to your mind,
write them in the appropriate columns, and then go back
and prayerfully consider what God is saying to you about
them. You will remember people from school and work,
people who were friends, and even people who made life
most difficult. You will walk back through events that at
the time seemed rather insignificant but that you now realize have helped shaped you. The opportunities you have
been given, whether or not you took them, will show you
the hand of God in your life. Your yearnings, the things
you long for, tell you where God has planted a dream and
a purpose for your future.

GOD'S HAND IN WRITING YOUR STORY

Consider some of the great people in biblical history.
Their experiences in life provided material for God to

write a great story with their lives. For example, the prophet Hosea's troubled marriage gave him the ability to paint a picture of God's relentless love for His wayward people. For Joseph, it was all the trouble that should have destroyed him but instead made him great that gave him the ability to assure centuries of God followers that He can take things others intend for your evil and use them for your good.

Moses had a considerably less-than-picture-perfect childhood. When he was just an infant, he had to be hidden to keep from being a victim of the mass murder decree announced for all Israelite baby boys under the age of two. Even though Pharaoh's daughter rescued him from death, he was taken from his parents' home to be raised. But later on, his story proved that God was in the process of giving him the best of both worlds. His mother (doubling as his nursemaid) taught him about almighty God, the One and Only. He learned reading and mathematical skills, legal maneuvers, leadership acumen, and military prowess in the palace of his adoptive mother. His story is captivating and inspiring, and insights gleaned from his account have changed millions of lives.

Nothing in these men's lives was wasted. The same is true for you and me. The heartbreak of my broken engagement, my athletic experiences, and my health issues (cancer, heart attack, and quadruple bypass surgery) are just a few of the hooks in my life God's used so I could start sharing my story. When you decide to look at your life with the prayerful desire to share your story to benefit others, God will give you insider's tips of what He was up to in your life all along.

GIVING OTHERS WHAT YOU HAVE

Once you have a perspective on the hand of God in your life—where you have been, what you are learning now, and what you want to do for and with God because of your gratitude—you have much to share with others.

Using words is the basic way of sharing your story, and the next critical step is getting an audience of people and holding their attention. This doesn't mean you get an agent and start booking gigs and interviews for yourself. You may never speak before hundreds or thousands at a church service or tell your story on a national broadcast, but that doesn't mean you can't take advantage of the opportunities in the time and space you *have been given* to impact people within your sphere of influence. Every one of us can have a huge impact when we look for opportunities to share our story.

Picture what can happen when sharing your story becomes part of your lifestyle. Everyone you meet is a potential audience with an "only God" need, and God is absolutely committed to causing your path to intersect with those who need what you have to offer. You just have to be alert, aware, and available.

You will get to verbally share your story when you

look for opportunities, when you look for people in situations that mirror where you have been or who have interests you share. Once you start thinking that everyone needs what you have, finding opportunities to share will not be your problem. You will practically fall over people in your path.

The Bible tells us to be prepared when we meet people who need what we have, who want to hear our story: "But in your hearts revere Christ as Lord. Always be prepared to give an answer to everyone who asks you to give the reason for the hope that you have. But do this with gentleness and respect" (1 Pet. 3:15 NIV). Peter was a follower of Jesus who absolutely made Christ Lord of his life. His decision to be a willing participant in the adventure with Christ turned around his character and made him a source of amazement to people who knew the before and after. All throughout his obedient and risk-taking adventure, he attracted audiences for his story—sometimes one or two at a time, sometimes thousands. He didn't have to aggressively force himself on anyone; he found curious and hungry listeners asking for an explanation for his changed life.

Every person who lives an "only God" life and has a grateful, willing heart for sharing will have that experience. The biggest difficulty many people have is adhering to Peter's instruction to share the story "with gentleness and respect"—or keeping people listening once they begin sharing. One friend told me that once she was thirty seconds into a sharing opportunity, she felt like her hoped-for listeners hit the MUTE button. They start checking their BlackBerrys and avoiding eye contact. She knows they are drifting off.

You can maximize your opportunities to tell your story by avoiding these major mistakes:

Not listening. Ernest Hemingway, obviously a great communicator, once said: "I like to listen. I have learned a great deal from listening carefully. Most people never listen." Don't be like most people. No one likes feeling that you are simply waiting for them to be quiet so you can have your say. So be a good listener. Put your own ego on hold, and really listen to what people are actually saying.

When you make an effort to really listen, you will pick up on people's needs, interests, and concerns, which will give you several potential paths for connecting your story with their lives. Ask questions that can't be answered with yes or no. For instance, if you are having a one-on-one conversation and someone mentions that his or her mother died a few months ago, you might ask, "Was it sudden or expected? I'm very sorry for your loss. How are you handling it?" When you ask questions that show genuine concern for people's situations, they will likely respond with more information to work with and more paths for you to choose from as you share what you really want to say.

If at first they answer your question with something

like, "Oh, I don't know," don't give up. Give them time, and gently prod just a little more. Remember, everyone's favorite story is his or her own. If you listen to a person's heart, you will capture his or her attention for *your* heart. The better you listen, the better you'll be listened to.

This approach works in groups, too. When I am scheduled to speak and share my passions somewhere, I always try to arrive early so I get a feel for the setting and the people. When I mingle and talk to the people who will shortly be my audience, I get clues for how to tailor what I have to say to walk through the doors that are open.

Letting anxiety get the best of you. Assume rapport with your target audience. Remember that you have the greatest information in the universe, and everyone you run into needs to know it. Assume they will care. Act as though the conversation you are having will bless the person you are talking to, and imagine that person will be, if he or she isn't already, one of your really good friends. It is always easier to be relaxed and engaging when you talk to your friends. No matter how large the crowd, imagine you are talking to one person. Not only does this lower your anxiety, it makes the sharing more direct and effective.

Poor delivery. Did you know that more arguments occur over the tone of voice than over what is actually said? One of the most important things in a conversation you want to be significant is not what you say, but how you say it. So slow down. Don't talk too fast. Speak with emotion, not in monotone. Make your voice a vehicle for your feelings. Work on your body language so that it matches the confidence of your voice.

Arguing. When you approach a conversation as if you have to prove you are right, most people are going to tune you out. The wise man *was* right; often when you win an argument, you lose the person. Remember you are a witness telling a powerful, life-changing story, not a prosecuting attorney trying to make a case.

Monopolizing the spotlight. Ouch! I've been guilty of this more times than I'd like to remember. My wife sometimes signals me when I'm crossing this line. It's important when you are trying to share your story to find a balance between listening and talking. Don't interrupt another's opinion, anecdote, or their view on what you are sharing. A young preacher expounded on and on to the dozen or so gathered for Bible study, some fighting sleep, others restless. Finally, an elderly man spoke up: "Son—this is a group Bible study. But it *is* a group, and we don't need to take on the whole Bible in one night."

Speaking critically or negatively. Criticizing others, using religious buzzwords, expressing political preferences, dwelling on your own disappointments and hurts—these all suck the positive energy out of most opportunities for you to share your most important story. Make sure that "gentleness and respect" become defining characteristics in your conversations.

Now that I've given you a list of mistakes to avoid when you want to tell your story, here are four things you should always try to do when you know you have an audience:

1. *Read the room.* Ask yourself whether it's a good time and place to say what you want to say. Forcing the *wrong* opportunity may make it certain that you will never get the *right* opportunity. Talking more and more about something people are unprepared or unwilling to hear will not change anyone's story. A good, simple piece of advice is, "When talking isn't helping, stop talking."

2. *Listen—really listen.* Whenever you feel someone isn't listening to you, try listening first. Really, truly listen. Give the person your undivided focus, ask curiosity-based questions (not argumentative ones), and summarize back to him or her the main points of what you believe he or she said. When you do this, you are communicating openness and respect in a very powerful way, and you are also teaching people how to listen to you. (By the way, parents, this is a great way to improve communication with your children.)

3. Cut to the chase. Don't overexplain or offer disclaimers, such as, "You may not want to hear this, but. . ." Before you begin talking, slow down and reflect to make sure you know what you want them to receive in this moment. Then, paint a clear, vivid picture with compelling word pictures and energy.

4. Absolutely tell the truth. When we exaggerate or embellish in hopes of helping another person make a decision, we may get a short-term convert or follower. This often results in long-term disillusionment and undermines your integrity. The truth is that most of the people God places in your life to hear your story are just like you and me—ordinary people. And like you, when they strive for an "only God" story, they can change their own lives and then change their world. When we share, we need to communicate the whole story—the good and the bad. "Compelling" does not mean embellished; it means something that resonates with the hearers. You can tell an accurate story without dishonoring anyone. Only the real truth honors God.

Another thing real truth telling does is create connection. Every human being longs to be connected with other people who are just like them. When you tell a story people can believe, and you tell it well, they are more likely to make the choices you suggest and invest in the things that matter to you.

MAKING REAL CONNECTIONS

You may be just the person and have just the story God will use to change a life and a direction. Telling how God has used your successes, troubles, opportunities, and relationships—the good and the bad—to bring you to Himself and transform your life is an incredible adventure.

The apostle Paul told his friends in Thessalonica that he went further than just *telling the story*. He wrote to them, "Because we loved you so much, we were delighted to share with you not only the Gospel of God but *our lives as well*" (1 Thess. 2:8 NIV, emphasis added). If you follow Paul's example, the next phase of changing the world through your story is actually *inviting people into your life*.

Paul planted a church in Thessalonica and wanted to see a corner of the world transformed through the propulsion of changed lives there. Though he shared the Gospel of God though powerful words, he was convinced that simple preaching was not enough. He was not just a teacher or preacher pontificating from a lofty pinnacle; he mingled closely, living life with these people he loved. He actually described himself in chapter 2 as being as closely involved with them as a nursing mother is with her infant child.

Patty and I have four children. I deeply cherish my role in their lives as father and would never want to replace it with any other responsibility. Still, I have never seen anything that compares to a nursing mother's connection with her child. She actually imparts her own life to the child. She eats food, processes it, and feeds it to the child she holds in her embrace. No wonder that the phrase, "The hand that rocks the cradle rules the world," written in the nineteenth century by the American poet William Ross Wallace, has evolved into a truism in our language.

We know nothing can eradicate the influence of a mother. But sharing your story up close and personal by sharing your actual life, the way a mother shares herself with her child, is to take an active hand in changing the world. Example is the most powerful teacher in the world. Dr. Howard Hendricks explains how example works: "You can impress people from a distance, but you can only impact them close up."

Every great movement of God in my life has been preceded by an invitation from someone (who was already writing a great story) to join them. They fed me what they had taken in and allowed me to be part of their ongoing journey. They poured into me what God had poured into them; they encouraged, educated, and inspired me to grow in my walk with Christ and become more than I imagined I could be. In doing that, they lit a fire in me.

AN INVITATION THAT CHANGED EVERYTHING

I was weeks away from starting my sophomore year of college, thinking I was going to be a high school teacher and coach, when God began wrecking my plans. I had an uncomfortable sense that He was calling me to do something else—specifically prepare for ministry.

I couldn't fathom a change in plans like that. Into that space walked Mike Walters, a young teacher and the coach of an Ohio Christian University basketball program in its infancy. Coach Walters asked me to transfer to OCU and help him build the basketball program there. At the last minute, I accepted the invitation, and everything changed forever for me. We did build the program. My second year there was our first season in the National Christian College Athletic Association. We went to the NCCAA Nationals, setting a few records along the way. And God built me. Coach Walters and others I met at OCU invited me into their stories, built into my life, and gave me the opportunity to write an adventure of my own.

Coach Walters became an example to me of what it takes to make a difference in another person's life, namely truly sharing yourself with him or her. Here is what I'm talking about:

Be there. When you invite someone into your story, in order to help them grow you must make a commitment to *be present.* You know what I mean—engaged, not talking a game you aren't actually playing. That nursing mother Paul mentioned didn't hand off her child to a babysitter but remained deeply and personally engaged.

When you invite someone into your story with the intent of growing them, you have to make presence a priority—meaning being available for instruction, encouragement, and accountability.

And playtime, too. Have some fun along the way with the people in your story line. You don't have to be all business to write an amazing story. Get together with people for dinner. Go play putt-putt golf or something else fun. These times make for great memories, they build strong relationships, and they let people know they aren't just a means to an end but that you value them as people and as friends. The conversations and life changing that will take place as you share your life will be among the most profoundly impacting.

Give support. You must *be supportive.* As people you have invited into your story grow and change, they will often contribute their own ideas. When they do, privately and publicly support, encourage, and praise them. Work with them—plan together, pray together, lead together. Let them receive credit and recognition for their contributions to the story. It will motivate them to write with bold strokes.

Be proactive. People will do not just what they are taught to do but what they see others doing. Your biological children are not the only ones who will bear your imprint. Anyone who gets close enough to another person to teach him what significance is really all about and how to make a difference will play a huge role in changing the world. Train those who have joined your story, model a changed life for them, and give them plenty of opportunity to practice what they have seen in you and learned from you. As they grow, they will begin world-changing adventures of their own.

SHARING YOUR STORY BY SHARING YOUR DREAMS

You can also share your story and activate momentum that will truly change the world by sharing your *yearnings*. Yearnings are the dreams God plants within your heart, the passions that move you, the things you are willing to sacrifice, sweat, and struggle for to make them happen. These are the things that are truly bigger than you, the things you realize in your deepest part will only happen if you experience "only God" moments.

For me, this is the most exciting phase of sharing my story. For many years, I have verbally shared the story God is writing in my life and helped others find the transforming grace of God to change their own stories. I have continually shared my life with people through relationship and example. Now I am seeing the explosively exponential effects of strategically inviting people to invest in my "only God" dreams.

It's exciting to share my journey with Christ and help others see the resulting changes in their stories. It is absolutely amazing to share my life in relationships that change both me and them. But verbally sharing my story comes with an element of risk, namely the risk that the audience may debate or even reject my beliefs and my story. The risk goes up another notch, too, because I put my heart on the line when I allow people to get close enough for me to share my life.

Without a doubt, however, the most heart-thumping, adrenaline-pumping risks I ever take is to share my yearnings, my dreams, my God-given passions with someone who has the capacity to help me and to ask that person to join me in changing the world.

This part of the adventure keeps me totally dependent on God. I am reminded to depend on Him every time I ask someone to take a leap of faith and buy into something unproven but so big only God can accomplish it. When I do that, I am giving someone an opportunity to first believe in my integrity and that I have done my homework, and then to believe that God has spoken to me and is now speaking to them through me. I never get past how weighty all that really is. However, I also never get past the greater facts that God has put these yearnings in my heart for a reason, and that the greatest thing I can do for myself and for others is to be obedient to Him.

THE COURAGE JUST TO ASK. . . AND HOW TO DO IT

Some years back, I attended a Willowcreek Leadership

Summit, where I listened as Bill Hybels passionately challenged church leaders to "make the ask"—to boldly, passionately, and aggressively ask people to join us in fulfilling God's mission and dream. (Side note—Bill is a living example of his message. On a daily basis, Willowcreek Church and the Willowcreek Association change the world through hundreds of thousands of leaders they train to be world changers. The unprecedented ways Hybels and Willowcreek have impacted the church world and the way we reach the secular world is only possible because he takes the risk of asking businesspeople and leaders in every field to help him fulfill what "only God"—through a group of people—can do.)

Bill Hybels shared the story of his father, an over-the-top successful businessman and a Christ follower who was never challenged to invest his considerable gifts—his skills, his service, and his finances—to change the world. Bill said his father never knew the significance and fulfillment that can come only from these above-and-beyond investments. With tears streaming down his face, emotion choking his voice, Bill pled something like this: "The church operating as it should is the hope of the world. No matter what their contributions are in other arenas of life, the most significant thing the people you know will ever do is join with others in changing the world. Their highest and proudest moments will come from laying what they have on the line for the purpose and cause of Christ. Don't cheat them by never asking." That moment and that message were carved into my heart. I decided I would do everything I could to grow deep enough and strong enough that God could trust me with His dreams for my one and only life—deep enough and strong enough that I could share with every prospect God put in my sphere of influence opportunities to be significant and to participate in "only God" ventures.

It is rare for a week to pass when I don't share my "only God" story and my "only God" dream with someone and "make the ask." My radar is always up, searching for a signal that a particular person I meet may be someone God has brought into my life to be part of the team it takes to do the "only God"–size task of changing the piece of the world He has given us.

When I receive a signal, I ask that person for an appointment. I don't go home and pray and prepare for an appointment I hope to secure; I ask for it right then and there. I come to the appointment covered in prayer and prepared to make good use of this person's time. I make it a point to be brief and to the point, and to present all the information needed to make a good decision. I ask the person to consider investing his time, skills, or resources in what God is doing. I have found that this is absolutely essential in making a successful request.

It is vital that you are prepared to clearly and specifically define the job God has assigned to you. You must know exactly what you need and want, and you must be prepared to competently present your request or proposal in a moment's notice.

People with a track record of personal success are the kind you need to ask for help with your "only God" yearnings. People with the ability to help you have gotten where they are through wisdom. They do not trust people who are timid in presenting their dreams or whose dreams are inconsistent or poorly shaped. If you can't instantly present and define the great dream you want to fulfill for God, if you can't explain why it is priority and lay out the path to making it happen, then you are not ready to ask people to invest their time, energy, and resources. If you want to be an explosive world changer who sees his big dreams come true, you are going to have to become comfortable sitting with the people to whom God has led you and ask them to invest in your dream.

God has led me to literally hundreds of opportunities to say, "I am so thrilled that God has blessed you with so much. I want to ask you to consider investing some of what He has given you into this dream He has given me. Together we can change this community."

One of the stories that has most influenced my life is the Genesis record of Joseph. You recall that God used an "only God" mix of trials and blessings to put Joseph in a unique place at a time of unprecedented national and cultural challenge. Pharaoh appeared to have the power, control, and resources, but he was impotent to save him and his nation in the time of drought and famine. God raised up Joseph, a man who did not covet what Pharaoh had but rather had what Pharaoh needed: the wisdom that only comes from a pure and direct connection with almighty God. Without Joseph's presence and wisdom, the famine would have been so great that the people wouldn't even remember their days of prosperity and hope. With Joseph's help, the culture prospered, and Joseph's family and personal dreams advanced as well.

I am convinced God has called and equipped me to be a Joseph, to speak to the Pharaohs of our region—people who have affluence and influence but do not know how to use them for eternal purposes. But I don't believe I am alone. I believe God is inviting every Christian leader to be a Joseph in these critical days of cultural famine and drought of wisdom and holiness.

Your story is unique and powerful. But God hasn't worked in you and with you just to have you to stop there. He wants you to share your story broadly and see what He can do to change the world. Step up to the challenge! God has brought you to this place and time for His eternity-shaking purpose.

ACTION STEPS

1. Make sure to put together your personal storyboard. Once you do, look at the things God has already written into your life that are just waiting to be processed and shared.

2. With whom are you sharing not only the Gospel, but your very life? What is your goal in sharing your life, and how are you working toward it?

3. What is your "only God" yearning, the place where you need investors of time, energy, and resources to accomplish it? Work on your dream and presentation until you can present it in one well-written page or in one five-minute window. Make a list of three people to whom you will "make the big ask" in the first three months after you are prepared.

8

{ Leveraging Your Story to Change the World }

Remember eighth-grade science class? Along with studying frogs and flowers, learning the names and distances of the planets, we learned about the world's "seven simple machines." I don't remember the details of those classes, but I recall that the wheel, the pulley, and the inclined plane are three of the simple machines central to developing civilizations. The lever was another one of those machines. A lever bar exerts a force to move a load by turning on a pivot or fulcrum. I remember an experiment in which I placed a triangular block at different points along a board and then measured the height and weight I could move at the end of the board.

The word *lever* was originally a noun, but over the years both "lever" and "leverage" have migrated across to business and language usage and morphed into both adjective and verb. One can't be in a business, motivational, or inspirational setting very long without hearing multiple mentions of "leverage."

But what does that mean to those of us who are writing our stories today?

The *American Heritage Dictionary of the English Language*, usually the most reliable guide to migrating word usage, provides only definitions for the word *leverage* as a noun—as in "power to act effectively" or "positional advantage." That means using resources for strategic advantage. But when we say we are "leveraging" our story, we mean we are making a conscious decision to use what we have to effectively change our position.

Anyone with the help of an almighty, loving God can do that. My sister frequently quotes this axiom: "Though no one can go back and make a brand-new start, anyone can start from now and make a brand-new ending." The message of our faith has always been that it is never, ever too late to turn things in a different direction. You cannot erase what happened in the past, but you can respond differently in the future and learn from what you have already been through. As amazing and wonderful as that is, it is also true that followers of Jesus Christ can even go further than just making the future different and better. God helps us "leverage" even the debris of our past, the hurtful things that have happened to us or the bad choices we have made, to effectively change our world.

Wilma Mast is one of our church's most valued leaders. Her "only God" story impacts thousands who also endured a painful beginning. Here is Wilma's story in her own words:

> *Some people have childhoods they remember fondly. Others have childhoods they need to recover from. I am still in the process of recovery. My childhood was filled with abuse. By the time I was twelve years old, I was cutting and praying to God to please allow me to die. By fourteen I was bulimic. At sixteen I was smoking, drinking, and doing drugs whenever possible. I was filled with hatred. I hated the people who abused me. I hated my parents for not protecting me. I hated them for not allowing me to go to high school. I hated the fact that I had to get two jobs to support the family. I hated my dad for being an alcoholic and my mom for falling apart. More than anything I hated myself. It was clear to me, I was unlovable.*
>
> *I spent my every waking moment trying to kill the pain that comes from living in hatred. I wanted to turn to God, but there was a huge obstacle between me and Him. Every single person who abused me was in church on Sunday. I started to see God as a part of that abuse. I walked away from God and that church. I said, "If those*

people are Christians, I will burn in hell."
I meant it. I had confused the actions of a
small group of people who went to church
every Sunday with the actions of an all-
powerful God.

The next years were an all-out effort to
destroy myself. The abuse others had inflicted
on me, I was now inflicting on myself. I
thought of suicide daily. My addictions
intensified and became consuming. When I
gave up on God and His people, there was
very little left to live for. Each day I would
come up with a reason to do that day.

Thankfully, God didn't leave me when I
left Him. One morning when I was driving
past a tree I had chosen as the one I would
eventually drive into, I heard a voice. It
was almost audible, and it said one of the
most beautiful phrases I have ever heard:
"I have designed you for greatness." I was
stunned. Why would God say such a thing
to me? There was nothing good in me! Why
greatness? I had no value, much less great
value. Yet, there was a glimmer of hope.

It took me ten years to fully come back to
God. There were many significant moments
along the way. One was the day I forgave
the abuse of my childhood. Forgiveness is

still the most powerful peace-bringing force in my world. The day I forgave was the first time I fully felt God's love. God's love is like nothing else in this world; it is pure, unconditional, and never ending. The miracle I have experienced and want to make sure you don't miss is this: His love flows through us. This fact has saved my life.

I have made it my goal in life to allow God to love people through me. I have told hundreds of people I love them. I have hugged hundreds more. I cannot count the people who have invited Christ into their lives because I asked them if they would like to. I started a mentor program that is now one hundred and fifty strong. We have collectively mentored hundreds of people.

There is no end to God's love. Give it away freely. It will change your life and the lives of everyone you come into contact with. I have tried hatred, and I have tried love. I will always choose love.

Changing the world was not a new thought for Blake Wood. He actually dreamed of doing just that, and he had some ideas how he would do it:

When I was eighteen years old, I was idealistic and wanted to change the world. Preparing to pursue a career path with the Marine Corps, I had earned a full scholarship through the Marine Corps to Penn State. Weeks before I was to start at Penn State and the ROTC (Marine Corps Option) program, my entry medical report came back. I was disqualified from the Marine Corps and from the scholarship. My world was seriously rocked. During this time of crisis and confusion, God's call on my life became clear, and I began to focus on pursuing the adventure God had in store for me.

Fast-forward a decade...

I had pastored and planted churches for the past ten years. My wife and I had married six years earlier, and we had been unable to have children. We were told that we were infertile. It was clear to us that God wanted us to be parents, and we began to pursue adoption. God opened the door for us to adopt an abandoned child in Moscow, Russia.

Our last day at the orphanage in Moscow, the director told us that our new daughter was not from Russia but from a neighboring central Asian country that is more than 99 percent Muslim. Back in the U.S., I did some research and found out that my daughter was from an ethnic group that had fourteen million people but only fifty known Christ followers at the time. I couldn't get that reality out of my mind as I fell deeper in love with our daughter. I was struck by the scandal of the fact that nearly two thousand years after Jesus told His followers to witness to people of every ethnic group, there were distinct groups, like my daughter's, with essentially no Gospel witness.

Fast-forward a decade. . .

I began to sense a deepening call to step down from my role as a local church pastor and move my family overseas to the Muslim-dominated Middle East. I knew that ministering in the Middle East and a Muslim context, like my daughter's home group, was going to be more than I could do alone. I reached out to Pastor Dwight Mason and NewPointe Church, because I knew of their heart to change the world. Together, we began to build a partnership, later known as Impact Middle East, and my family and I moved to Amman, Jordan, at *the end of 2001.*

For the next ten years I was involved in sharing the Gospel, helping people follow Jesus more faithfully, and empowering national leaders to carry the good news of Jesus throughout their nations. The result of God's empowerment of these efforts has been the formation of well over three hundred new "Christ Communities"—hundreds of house churches as well as about a dozen more traditional church models.

In December of 2003, on my third trip into Baghdad that year, I stood in a worship service in a church plant that we had launched shortly after Saddam Hussein was deposed. I was struck by the irony of the moment. There were marines throughout that city and I, if I had followed my chosen path, would have likely been there wearing the uniform of the Marine Corps. Instead, I was being used to not simply "change the world" but to "change eternity."

Though the names and experiences of each story are unique, I know hundreds of people whose story lines include many of the same elements as the ones above. I know many whose stories have dark chapters the characters never planned to write, chapters they wish they could edit out or gloss over when they recount their history. Their choices and mistakes haunted them until they chose to pick up the pen and write a new life story. "Mary" did that, and she writes with gratitude and joy:

> *Our life is a living testimony to a loving God. We are proof positive that He can turn even the ugliest event into a glorious miracle of His goodness.*
>
> *I knew from the moment I first saw "Pete" that I wanted to spend the rest of my life with him. He was visually perfect to me—tall, dark, and handsome to be sure. As I grew to know him I found him pretty attractive on the inside as well. He accepted my daughter as his own, and we were married eighteen months later. It wasn't long before we were blessed with two wonderful boys. My life was great. . .or so I thought.*
>
> *Christ was not the center of our marriage. He was not the center of our anything. Frankly, He had no place in our lives whatsoever. Drugs and alcohol were the things we worshipped. We had that in common from the very beginning. We went to work, we took care of the children, and we partied. . .hard at times.*
>
> *After ten years of this lifestyle, evil*

erupted like an active volcano in our lives and blew the entire family apart. The event left me a single mom—again—with an ex-husband in prison, and tongues wagging at every turn. It was the worst time of my life by far. I was so very broken.

"Pete" got saved in prison and tried his best to get through to me. My heart was hard, and I withheld forgiveness. I was angry. I deserved to be angry, and I intended to remain angry forever. That was my life plan. Anytime I felt my love for Pete begin to rise up inside of me, I drowned it with alcohol. Satan had me convinced that I could never forgive him, never trust him, never love him, and never take him back. After all, what would people think?

After doing eighteen months of a three-year sentence, Pete was released for good behavior. He kept speaking to me about being a new man, but I was still hangin' with Satan and believing all his lies.

One day, I called Pete over to tell him that I had gotten a DUI. But the words "I still love you" are what came out of my mouth instead. I was shocked. The instant I spoke those words, I was set free. I still get emotional when I go back to that moment.

Pete and I embraced and cried and laughed and yelled and felt God in the middle of us for the first time ever. Pete led me through the sinner's prayer, and I was saved! Now life was truly good.

As we moved to reconcile our family, my then twenty-year-old daughter had a son. Due to poor choices on her part, he was removed from her custody and placed in foster care. Pete and I wanted to be a part of his life. We asked the courts for visitation, and the judges agreed to give it to us. Job and Family Services strongly disagreed and asked for another judge to step in. Pete and I gathered a dozen or so letters from different individuals attesting to the people we had become, and that was not *the people Job and Family Services saw on paper. The second judge reviewed the letters, listened to arguments, and ultimately agreed with the first judge's ruling. We were allowed to be a part of our grandson's life.*

Two years later, my daughter had a baby girl. The day after she was born, Job and Family called me and asked if I wanted that baby. I just could not believe it. Within a month, we had her brother with us as well. Only God could pull off a plan such

> *as this. He gets all of the glory, for without*
> *Him we are those people on that paper.*
>
> *It has been four and a half years since*
> *we obtained custody of those two precious*
> *babies, and we vowed to bring them up in*
> *the ways of the Lord. We were also blessed*
> *with a second chance to do the right thing by*
> *our own children as well. We don't always*
> *get it right, but with Christ as our founda-*
> *tion we can't go wrong.*

These are just a few of the amazing "only God" stories I have personally heard. I could tell you about Jerry Anderson, who was broken financially, relationally, and spiritually. As he connected with God, he met John Schrock, another man with an "only God" story. Today these men are touching the world through the LaRed organization, which teaches the transformative power of values in prisons, schools, and governments.

I could share Edna Brubaker's story. In heaven now, Edna was a wife and mother who was convinced that every child needed a Christian education. Not at all defeated by the fact that that biblical principles could no longer be taught as public school curriculum, she pursued the idea of "release time." Thousands of children benefitted. Over forty years, a minimum of five hundred children a year were her students.

Paul Weaver would tell you that in the 1970s he

was bankrupt and on the verge of ruin. But he had the bodacious faith to say to God, "If You will help me, I will never forget You." God honored his business and multiplied his investments beyond belief. I challenged many successful businessmen in our community: "Now that you have had personal success, why don't you do something that is an adventure? Do a start-up company, and give all the proceeds to ministry." Paul is the only one who has taken me up on it—and you can believe that his new story is changing the world. All of these people are part of an exciting fellowship of "formerly ordinary." Anyone can be *ordinary* and do the *ordinary*—but no one can be ordinary and safe and do the *extraordinary*. Extraordinary requires deliberate choice to write a new story and then to share that story with the world. Once you choose the steps of faith and obedience, you truly can work with God to change the world.

WHY YOU'RE QUALIFIED

After reading the stories I've included in this chapter, you might still be thinking, *I'm not sure I could actually be a world changer*. But think about this: the greatest heroes in the Bible were people we likely would not have put on our "short list" of candidates to excel.

Remember Noah? He got drunk and humiliated himself. Abraham was old and lied under pressure, and his grandson Jacob followed in his footsteps and was a liar and a schemer. In a world that prized beauty, Leah was not beautiful, Joseph didn't get along with his brothers, Moses was timid and stuttered, Gideon was afraid and untrained, Rahab was a prostitute, Timothy and Jeremiah were too young to get respect, David committed adultery and then ordered a murder to cover it up, Elijah suffered from depression, Jonah ran from obedience, Naomi was a widow, Job went bankrupt, Peter denied Christ, the disciples fell asleep when Jesus needed them most, Martha worried about everything, the Samaritan woman had multiple divorces and lived with a man to whom she wasn't married, Zacchaeus was short and sneaky, Paul was a self-righteous persecutor, Timothy had physical issues, and Lazarus was dead.

Yet, God found a way to use every single one of those people. And He did that by changing them from the inside out.

Take the apostle Paul, for instance. He is one of history's most changed men. He was a murderer, a persecutor of Christians, and the self-defined "worst of all sinners." But he came to a fork in the road and made the life-altering choice to follow Jesus, the One he had once maligned and opposed. The new story he wrote is still changing the world to this day. He actually wrote most of the New Testament and gives every person who feels inadequate insight and encouragement to move beyond the ordinary:

Take a good look, friends, at who you were

when you got called into this life. I don't see many of "the brightest and the best" among you, not many influential, not many from high-society families. Isn't it obvious that God deliberately chose men and women that the culture overlooks and exploits and abuses, chose these "nobodies" to expose the hollow pretensions of the "somebodies"? That makes it quite clear that none of you can get by with blowing your own horn before God. Everything that we have—right thinking and right living, a clean slate and a fresh start—comes from God by way of Jesus Christ. That's why we have the saying, "If you're going to blow a horn, blow a trumpet for God."

1 Corinthians 1:26–31 msg

ACTION STEPS

1. Take a look at someone you know whom God is really using. Ask that person to sit down with you and discuss his life choices. Ask him to identify the changes God made in him so He could use him.

2. If you know God is already using you, identify and chronicle what steps of obedience have been most important to you in writing your story. Find someone with whom to share your story.

3. Identify some current areas of risk and change God might be challenging you to explore.

9

{ Helping Your Children
Write a Great Story }

Author and preacher Erwin McManus tells the story of his young son's return from his very first church summer camp. McManus assumed it would be a great adventure full of warm memories, but eight-year-old Aaron returned a frightened child. He wanted to sleep with the lights on in his room and didn't want his father to leave. It seems the teen counselors had entertained their young campers with demon tales.

"Pray for me, Daddy," Aaron tearfully pled, head buried in the pillow. "Pray that God will make me safe."

His father breathed deeply and said, "Son, I just can't do that. I love you too much to pray that God just makes you safe. I will pray that God will make you dangerous—so dangerous that when you walk into a room, all the demons will run away!"

In a moment, Aaron responded, "Okay, Dad. Then pray that God makes me really, really dangerous!"

I don't know what the Lord has called Aaron Mc-Manus to do and be, but I have a sense his story is going to be world shaking simply because his father started prepping him for greatness from a very young age.

Peter F. Drucker, the prolific, bestselling author of more than one hundred books, was frequently asked, "What is the best book you have written?" His standard answer was, "My next one!"

Parents who deeply love their children feel that way about their family story. Which chapter do we want to be the best of all? The next one, the chapter our children write. We can help them write a fearless story, one dangerous to the kingdom of darkness. But we need to start as early as possible.

THE IMPORTANCE OF STARTING EARLY AND WITH YOURSELF

George Barna's research, cited in his book *Transforming Your Children into Spiritual Champions*, indicates that a person's lifelong behaviors and views are generally developed when they are young—particularly before they reach the teenage years. Barna concluded that a person's moral foundations are generally in place by the time they reach age nine. His data indicated that, in most cases, a child's spiritual beliefs are irrevocably formed by about age thirteen.

Among American children, Barna found that a majority have made a lasting determination about how Christ's death and resurrection impacts them by age twelve. The research sampling of pastors, church staff, and lay leaders showed that more than 80 percent of those leaders had consistently been involved in a ministry to children for an extended period of years prior to age thirteen. Clearly, what we do matters when children are young.

I hope you took chapter 3 very seriously. Understanding your story, knowing how it impacts you and your entire family and future, and vigorously undertaking the task of breaking from the bonds that hinder you is the stepping-stone to helping you *and* your children succeed.

In her memoir *It's Always Something*, the late Gilda Radner profoundly, perhaps unintentionally, illustrates this parenting principle. Dibby, her childhood nanny/housekeeper, was a nurturing woman with whom Gilda was very close. She recounted how Dibby's cousin had a mutt that was expecting puppies in about a week. Just before the puppies were to arrive, the dog ran under a running lawnmower and lost her two back legs. Of course, they immediately rushed the much-loved dog to the vet, who gave them two options: They could put her to sleep, or he could sew her up and she would live and deliver the puppies. They chose the latter. The little dog healed quickly, and before she delivered the puppies, she taught herself to walk in a new way. She would take two steps with her front legs, and then flip her backside into the air. She would repeat this "step and flip" procedure until she got where she wanted to go. Gilda says, "She gave birth to six little puppies, all in perfect health. She nursed them and then weaned them. And when they learned to walk, they all walked like her."

Doesn't that describe families you know? Generation after generation pick up sick and inadequate ways of living, not because it is necessary or natural but because it is what they have seen and know how to replicate.

I hope you are working with God to break free of every bond and unhealthy pattern in your life, because giving your child a spiritually, emotionally, and relationally healthy parent is job number one in helping him or her write a great story. This is not a "one and done" process, either—it is a lifetime commitment to becoming like Christ. It is a daily commitment to humility, to receiving correction when you are wrong and putting the necessary changes into effect.

As life moves forward, God will even use your children to correct and shape you. Your attitude in receiving their input will either enhance or stall your growth, and theirs as well. My daughter Sarah is an intelligent and articulate communicator. When she was in junior high, she began correcting my word usage and poor grammar. Frankly, I had a choice to make. I could be defensive and annoyed, or I could be humble and grow. God helped me choose the latter so I could grow and receive what my daughter had to offer me. She learned to give input graciously, and I learned from someone I wouldn't have expected to teach me.

This peeling off of the old and unhealthy never stops. In a healthy body, old skin cells are washed away and new fresh ones replace them. Likewise, God intends for me to peel away the old layers of my life and keep growing and changing and becoming more and more transformed into the image of His Son (see Rom. 8:29). Committing myself to actively stay in that process is my first gift to my child's story.

BEING A HEALTHY PARENT

The second most significant contribution I can make to my child's story is giving my child a second parent who is healthy and growing. You may feel despair when you read that and think, *I could have used this information a long time ago! I can improve myself, but there's nothing I can do about my child's other parent.*

While it is very difficult to "improve" your spouse and make him or her the kind of parent who can move the children to write their own great stories, here's a common kind of story I have seen over the years: A young woman is attracted to a "bad boy" and gets caught up in the adrenaline-fired pursuit. Before long she is pregnant. The actual truth of who this young man is becomes visible even to her sometime after he discovers he's about to be a father. Then the girl and her family mount a strong campaign to keep the young man out of her life and away from the baby. This young man is not who she wants to be the father of her child. And yet he is. She got involved with him without a solitary thought about the impact he would have on any child she might bring into the world.

Of course, this goes both ways. Men can just as easily choose poorly. Even when the outcome is not as predictable or disastrous as our "story," it is all too rare for people to consider if the person who looks so compelling as a date will measure up as a parent. Shortly after my broken engagement, a man I greatly admired from my home church surprised and helped me by sharing an intimate peek into his own life. He said, "Dwight, I can tell you from personal experience there is something more important to your happiness and your future happiness than marrying a girl who is a Christian. I know generally everyone says that's most important, but you can marry a Christian and still be in a really hard place. I believe the most important thing is to marry a girl who has a good relationship, or at least a relationship she has personally resolved, with her father. If she doesn't, she will view you and life through that lens, and it's going to be a continual struggle for you and any children you have."

In his book *Date or Soul Mate?*, Dr. Neil Clark Warren says the powerful impact of emotional health cannot be overestimated. He said he has learned that too many people bring personal emotional difficulties into marriage, and when they do that, it's only a matter of time before the relationship goes south. He also estimates that in 75 to 80 percent of the marriages that end in divorce or separation one or both of the partners suffer from some sort of "emotional health deficiency."

So what is emotional health? Dr. Warren, perhaps best known as the founder of eharmony.com, an online service designed to help persons make wise choices in choosing life partners, says that emotional health begins with a well-constructed self-concept—knowing yourself well, being well defined as a person, and feeling good about yourself. An emotionally healthy person, Dr. Warren says, is free of addictions and character disorders and displays unselfishness, generosity, and truthfulness. This person is able to make wise, thoughtful decisions.

Dr. Warren sums it all up by saying that an emotionally healthy person is able to live life free from the drive to please any other man or woman, and that this freedom comes only from a radical experience of unconditional love from God.

When you get into a radical relationship with the God who loves you and made you, you become free to become the person you were created to be—your authentic self. Then you are able to love, parent, and set your child on an exciting journey. If you are not yet married, it is vitally important that you covenant to not get married until you *are* that emotionally healthy person and until you have found an equally emotionally healthy person.

But what if you already have children and the situation is less than optimal? Then do *whatever it takes* to get healthy. Go to counseling, read books, repent, humble yourself, pray, and fast. If you are no longer with your child's parent, for that child's sake, seek godly wisdom in making the now-broken relationship as free from hostility and as healthy as possible.

There is more help to become emotionally healthy available today than ever. There is no excuse for staying broken and hurting. Nothing you give your children can make up for the lack of healthy, growing, changing parents.

A BAKER'S DOZEN STEPS IN HELPING YOUR CHILD WRITE A GREAT STORY

As you make continual progress toward emotional health for yourself and for your marriage, you can make several other contributions to the development of your children's blockbuster story:

1. Help your children to embrace the art of accepting change and remaining flexible. While it is true that a child needs a certain amount of routine to establish stability, growing up with the sense that life revolves around "my schedule" and "my needs" will prove to be a great handicap. We have already established that change is difficult for most people, despite the fact that life is a continuous cycle of change. People who embrace change and remain flexible have a sizeable head start on the rest of the pack.

2. Dismiss cynical attitudes and sarcasm from your home. This requires constant vigilance, because much of today's humor comes from the darker side. But enough exposure to cynicism, even under the cover of humor, will warp your children's perspectives and put them at a disadvantage in a world that needs hope and optimism.

3. Give your children exposure to a diverse world. We live in a world filled with all kinds of people—people in different ethnic groups, belief systems, cultures...just to name a few of the ways people are different from one another. If you live in an area whose population is of mostly one race—like we do—do your best to intentionally broaden your children's friendships and experiences with all kinds of people. Athletic teams, camps, special skills lessons—all of these can be opportunities for your children to develop appreciation for differences and similarities in people.

4. Help your children develop a big and compassionate worldview. Take the time to talk with your children about world events and about our responsibility as Christians for meeting others' needs. If you can help your children develop compassion and concern for other people early, who knows what God may do in and through them? I learned this kind of compassion growing up myself. One of my most memorable Christmases with my family was when we all gave up our gift exchange and instead donated to a charity/mission. Our family refrigerator door was covered with pictures of people we, as a family, invested in—sponsored children, missionaries, and kids with medical needs, including some who needed surgeries for conditions such as cleft palates. Dad and Mom also helped raise money for three of us to go on mission trips. Today, all four of us, as well as our families, are deeply involved in compassionate service here and abroad, due in no small way to the fact that our parents taught us—through word and deed—how rewarding and fulfilling compassionate service can be.

5. *Give your children up-close-and-personal experiences with every great person you can.* My parents were intent on seeing that we met every missionary, servant of God, great businessperson, and contributor in the world we could. Our dinner table was the setting for many tales of adventure, sacrifice, and miracles as our guests shared first-person experiences from their own faith journeys. Mom and Dad did the extra work of hosting in our home, and we had many honorary aunts and uncles who became part of an extended heritage we never wanted to disappoint.

6. *Allow your children to know and understand the truth about consequences.* Children need to know that great people become great by the choices they make and that mediocre or lesser people get where they are by way of choices and consequences, too. Dad was an expert at teaching this truth in nonjudgmental and matter-of-fact

ways. The pastor's home often attracts people in need of food or other help, so a lot of down-on-their-luck people sat at our table, as well. We shared one dinner with a homeless alcoholic who smelled of his most recent indulgence and of life on the street. Dad treated him as a gentleman, spoke to him kindly, and introduced him to the family. I was a baby at the time, but I later found out my sisters were put off by his odor and appearance and were not at all eager to be close to him. After that dinner and conversation were finished, Dad led us in prayer with and for the homeless man, and then our visitor was on his way. Afterward, Dad walked around the kitchen, helped clear the table, and said to my sisters, "That poor man. One day he was a sweet, clean, happy little baby just like your brother. He never dreamed the first time he drank alcohol that he would end up losing his family and end up like he is." Period. That was it. That one moment of exposure to consequences did more to make my sisters wary of alcohol than any sermon ever could.

7. Work with God to balance grace and truth. Grace and truth are the ingredients we need for growth, but we tend to divide them one against the other. When we don't get it right, we have confused kids, some who are way too hard on themselves and the others who live freewheeling and irresponsible lives. We tend to practice one in a given season or moment or with a particular person. But we as followers of Christ can't choose between the two because we need both. To give your children the best start, you as a parent must learn to be graceful and truthful at the same time.

Grace means favor—unearned kindness simply shown as an act of love. Truth is reliable and trustworthy. When we give grace without truth, it ends up being "love without limits." When we give truth without grace, it becomes "limits without love." Children raised without a healthy dose of both tend to show it in their life choices. When a child leans more toward a "truth" parent, he'll generally end up being overly hard on himself and others. If he leans more toward a "grace" parent, he'll have a hard time living up to healthy, godly standards.

The child who receives great doses of love and grace, and great doses of limits and structure, gets a great start on life. Grace lets a child know how deeply and completely she is loved; truth guides her into the reality of what she must do and become. Grace and truth say, "I forgive you for what you did. But, here's the consequence we're facing." Grace and truth say, "I am 100 percent on your side, even if you don't feel like I am. But you have to respect the rules."

Grace and truth equip children to live well, so don't give one without the other. Great people know that grace means someone is pulling for them and on their team, and they know that truth is always *for* them, not *against* them.

8. Prioritize responsibility and self-control. Responsibility is probably best defined as the ability to own your own life and your own problems. I know that no matter what circumstance, situation, or problem I face, the buck stops with me. Responsible children know they are loved, valued, and cherished—but in the end, they also know that what happens to them and for them is up to them.

Parents who "hover" and who are too quick to fix their children's problems stunt their child's ability to "own" his or her life. Kids naturally hand their problems to their parents: "My room is messy—clean it," "My science project is due—build it," or "I got into trouble—get me out of it." One of the most important tasks you as a parent must tackle is transforming your child's perspective from "My life is *your* responsibility" to "My life is *my* responsibility."

Responsible people—people with the self-control to persevere and who behave according to their values instead of the emotions of the moment—are the ones who succeed in relationships, careers, missions, and in their overall life adventure. They know and live the axiom, "If it's going to be, it's up to me!" On the other hand, uncontrolled, irresponsible people muddle through life with an inner belief that somehow, somewhere, someone is about to come to the rescue and make their lives better.

When your child learns that the pen really is in his hand, he will be on his way to writing a great story. Keep in mind, though, that your child will likely initially have no interest in becoming responsible. Children are born sinners and have a tremendous natural bent to manipulate and control their parents into doing for them what they should be doing for themselves. At times, it may feel like love for the parent to take responsibility for something that the child should handle themselves. The reality, though, is that we are negating their chance for personal greatness.

9. *Teach your children to lose well. What?* you might be thinking. *Isn't this book about writing a great story?* Yes it is, but you still need to teach your child to lose well, because all of us lose sometimes. Every single one of us is flawed and imperfect, and we all lose, fail, and make mistakes from time to time.

As your child grows and develops, the pond will get deeper and the fish will get bigger. Your son won't always be the best player on the football team, and your daughter won't take every lead role. When Dad and Mom don't teach their children to take the losses and disappointments in stride but instead seek to explain why everyone else's decisions are wrong or unfair, they will not learn to live well in a world that sometimes disappoints.

Jesus promised us that we would indeed experience trouble and loss in this world. That's because sin and death entered the picture back in the Garden of Eden. But He also promised that He had overcome the world. When you help your children face loss and failure constructively, you help them write a story filled with life and joy—despite the difficulties every son of Adam and daughter of Eve endures.

10. Help your children develop a specific competence and poise. In order to have a great story, your child will eventually have to be accepted into the world of mature adults. It's not uncommon to see young people who initially looked like they had everything it takes to get a good start dribble out and never quite get to a good story. The reason often is that they got confused over unconditional love. They thought being loved excused them from the need to actually become competent in life. Sometimes we don't require enough from our children, because we are so focused on making them feel totally loved and accepted. Helping your child find areas where she can excel—a skill she can master—is a huge hand in the world of adults, where you have to know something to make it. Solomon said it well: "Do you see a man skilled in his work? He will stand before kings; he will not stand before obscure men" (Prov. 22:29 NASB). The relational aspect of skill mastery, doing it with personal poise and respect for others, catapults a person into a position of great opportunity. Sports, mechanical work, part-time jobs—helping your child find something he can do and then expecting him to persevere until he masters it is one of the most rewarding things you and your child will do together.

11. Make delayed gratification a priority lesson. We all desire pleasure and happiness, and there is nothing necessarily wrong with that. In fact, God made us for pleasure and happiness. It's normal and healthy for our children to desire gratification. But pleasure right now is not always possible or wise.

Do you remember the Marshmallow Test? It was a famous study done in the 1960s, in which researchers gave children a marshmallow and told them they could either eat it right then or wait until the researcher returned and have two marshmallows. When the researchers followed up on the children later, they found that those who were able to wait the fifteen minutes and get the second marshmallow had fewer behavioral difficulties, did better in school, and had fewer addictions. They discovered that the ability to delay gratification was actually a great indicator of how well the children would do later in life.

The inability to wait and work for good things is a stage of immaturity every successful person grows out of. Learning delayed gratification is an essential part of becoming great. Kids who go through life getting everything they want aren't at all prepared for coping with and facing the world, and they typically become dependent on someone or something else (such as an artificial substance) to help them cope.

You must teach your children patience and perseverance, that they can obtain certain things only by working for them and waiting for them. The inability to wait until the right time to buy a new car, or to wait until God can bless a sexual relationship, or to put in the discipline it takes to pass classes instead of party—these are the kinds of choices that short-circuit potentially amazing futures.

12. Make your family life fun and adventurous. Kids have an easier time resisting the lure of negative adventure when the story they get to write outshines anything else. Ask your kids for some wild and crazy dreams they would like to accomplish. Have everyone make a list of fun and exciting things they would like to do, and then go to work making those things happen. When your kids are pushing the envelope at home with your blessing, taking risks to do amazing things, they won't have the urge to act out and write a chapter they'll eventually wish wasn't part of their story.

13. Realize you can't do it alone. Someone once observed that "no other success can compensate for failure in the home." That statement should strike panic into the heart of every parent. It doesn't take too many days on the job for a dad to realize that the toolbox is missing a few tools to do the job he needs to do. And a mother's stress can overwhelm her when she sees she doesn't have all the ingredients for the meal she wants to prepare for her children.

Not a single one of us is equipped to do the monumental job of shaping and raising a child on our own.

All of us run out of time, energy, and resources. We don't have all the skills we need. But this is where one of God's greatest ideas comes in. The church, the family of God, is His gift to your family and mine.

When my father is complimented on the outcome of his and my mother's child-rearing efforts, he always says, "It took the influence of every godly person in the three churches we served to make our kids who they are." As our children grow and enter young adulthood, I find that I identify with Dad. The people of NewPointe, and God's family in general, have given our children much that Patty and I could never have provided on our own.

God has designed us to need and connect with others. When you get deeply involved in a great church and build positive relationships there, you open many doors of opportunity for your children. You will always be the greatest influence on your child, for good or for bad, but for their story to be great, they will need to have other positive influences and role models who enhance what you give them as well as fill in the gaps. Patty and I have discipled and built into people like Paul and Dondra Rothel. This relationship is one of God's proofs to me that when we sow generously, we reap generously. As the years went by, they chose to pour themselves into our daughter Sarah's life, starting in a kindergarten class. They entrusted her with leadership at a very early age and invested into her and another young girl outside official "church time" as well. Paul and Dondra laid an incredible foundation for ministry and service in their lives. Our daughter is now in college and is writing an incredible and impactful story of her own. I believe it all kicked into high gear when two adults outside of her family believed in her and gave her a place to serve and grow at the ripe old age of seven years. They added a dimension to her life we could not.

Think about your children as they are right now and then fast-forward twenty-five years. Your kids are grown, and everyone is home for a family reunion. What story do you want them to tell? What character traits do you want them to have? How satisfied do you hope they are with their lives? Your decisions today will have every-thing to do with the story told on that day. Help them write well. Nothing else you do will matter more.

ACTION STEPS

1. Take an honest look at your personal life as it is right now. What do you need to change in order to be a stronger asset in shaping your child's future? Prayerfully set a goal to grow in this area over the next six months, and plan a strategy to make the growth happen.

2. Assess the quality of your relationship with your child's other parent—whether or not you are married to that person. What can you do to improve the health of this relationship?

3. Honestly evaluate how your child is doing in laying a foundation for a great future; then seek God's wisdom for taking new steps in a positive direction. If you have an adult child you believe you have failed in any way, prayerfully plan a time to seek your child's forgiveness and ask how you can assist him or her now.

4. Write a letter to each of your children, expressing your confidence in them and your prayers for their future.

10

{ The Vision to Write a Great Team Story }

Writing a great story is never done without great effort. But it's like a lot of things in that it often seems easier to do it yourself—at least initially. It's easier to just run out and mow the yard than to teach your child to do it, easier to improve your golf game than to improve your basketball team. The challenges of building a cohesive championship team are many, so it can be tempting to be a lone ranger.

However, whether you lead a business, a sports organization, a church, or a nonprofit, the world is looking to you to build a great team story, one bigger than you can author alone. And that can't happen unless you gather very different people into an empowered and powerful team.

Our church is a proverbial melting pot of people. Every social group and church background is represented. A few here have never known any church but ours, while a few have been wounded by church fights and splits and ended up with us. Those veterans of church wars feared splintering and fighting here, too, and were concerned that the constant change and expansion would ruin this church, just like it had the ones they came from.

But through more than a quarter century of ministry, that has never happened. People have left, of course—some of them church leaders—but we have never had a split. I believe the primary reason we've remained together through all the change and growth is that we have had a vision big enough to draw us together and to utilize all our talents and dreams.

THE IMPORTANCE OF VISION

Vision dramatically increases the probability that you will act with purpose and actually end up where you were meant to be. Vision is the way dreams become reality. In order for a team to come together and accomplish great things corporately, its leader must clearly receive a vision from God that stirs his or her passion *and* enables others to see the end result long before it comes about.

Walt Disney's capacity for vision is legendary. He faced bankruptcy, professional ruin, and more rejection than you can imagine. But his vision was strong, real, and nonnegotiable—so he simply kept at it. Walt died before Florida's Walt Disney World opened. On opening day, a reporter commented to Walt's brother Roy that it was a shame that Walt did not live to see it. Roy quietly replied,

"He saw it. If Walt hadn't seen it first, we wouldn't be seeing it today."

Your first step in creating a great team, the kind of team that can change the story of your church or business, is asking for and receiving a clear and compelling vision from God that you are willing to invest everything you have to see fulfilled. You must ask yourself what vision gets you up in the morning and keeps you going all day. Until you have that kind of vision, team building will be slow and arduous, and it will likely fail. But when you have it, things begin to matter in a new way.

Once God has given you a dream for changing your personal story—and your part of the world—your next step is doing the "legwork" needed to build your team. So how can you successfully accomplish that? Read on!

THE NUTS AND BOLTS OF BUILDING A GREAT TEAM

The quality of people on your team will determine your team story's ceiling. In his book *Good to Great*, Jim Collins uses a bus analogy to make this very point about building a great team. Collins says you have to get the wrong people *off* the bus and the right people *on* the bus, and then get those right people in the right seats.

That's the place to start building your team. Choosing the right people and putting them in the right seats is the key to keeping yourself from having to pull over every few miles to reassign seats, settle squabbles, and make repairs.

But how can you know who the right people are? Whenever I have to make decisions about team members, I know it's important for me to minimize my personal emotions and opinions about people. That's why I follow this list of checkpoints:

Checkpoint #1—A Calling. When you are in the process of building a team, you have to ask yourself one simple question about every potential team member: Does this person have a calling to my vision? Nothing causes more stress and tension than differences in the size and nature of callings. If my calling is bigger or different from yours, my calling will likely irritate you. You may want to minimize what I believe we must do and be. You may see the things I know are essential as optional and a trouble to do.

It's like an adolescent whose dream job is to work at an amusement park simply because he is obsessed with the roller coasters he has ridden and the experience he has had there. One day, the young man is hired to work at the park. At first, thinking that working at the park guarantees him unlimited rides, he is over-the-top thrilled. After just a few days on the job, he gets edgy and restless and impatiently asks his boss, "When do we get to ride the rides?"

The boss answers, "Ride the rides? You didn't get hired to ride the rides! You are here *now* to create for *others* the experience that so impacted *you*."

Some people may want to work with you because they have enjoyed the ride so much, because they believe that being a part of your team will be a daily repeat of the thrill and excitement that drew them to your vision. However, it's possible that they don't have a calling to your vision, just to the excitement. When they don't have that calling, they can become dissatisfied with your vision and be a source of tension. However, if they do have a calling, they will commit all they have to seeing the vision become reality.

Checkpoint #2—Competency. A person's desire and calling are absolutely essential, but that does not negate the need for competency on the job. Your story will never get big enough to change your world unless the people on your team are actually capable of doing the job required.

Competency can be defined as the measure of a person's ability to do a particular job to particular standards. That might mean giving a person who has the ability but not the knowledge or the formal education to do a particular job the necessary training.

You will need to define the framework for competency for each position on your team, including the knowledge, skills, and attributes needed to perform the job well. This will help you hire well, and also protect people from the personal damage resulting from being hired beyond their competency. When you have that framework prepared, you will be able to assess, maintain, and monitor the knowledge, skills, and attributes of potential candidates for your team or organization.

Checkpoint #3—Capacity. Capacity is decidedly different from capability or competency. Capacity refers not to what I am capable and competent to do but to *how much* of that work I am able to handle. Increasing my capacity means expanding how much of a certain task I am able to manage.

Jesus spoke of the differences in personal capacity when He told the story of the servants and their talents (see Matt. 25:14–30). The parable included the stories of a one-talent man, a two-talent man, and a five-talent man. The number of talents these men were given did not determine their innate personal value, but it did determine what the master expected of them and what they were able to produce.

Scripture tells us that each of us should have a correct estimation of ourselves, including our capacities. *The Message* translation of Galatians 6:4–5 reads: "Make a careful exploration of who you are and the work you have been given, and then sink yourself into that. Don't be impressed with yourself. Don't compare yourself with others. Each of you must take responsibility for doing the creative best you can with your own life."

Different people have different capacities for the work they are called to do. Giving them responsibilities that are beyond their capacities can be overwhelming personally and destructive corporately. A leader's responsibility includes helping his or her team members discover their capacities, allowing them to live and work within them, and encouraging them to do their "creative best" with what they have been given.

Checkpoint #4—Character. In his book *From Third World to First,* author Lee Quan Yew, prime minister of Singapore from 1959 to 1990, wrote of his appointment of ministers in the government: "The attrition rate was high because, despite all the psychological tests, we could never accurately assess character, temperament, and motivation."

We can define character as an individual's bundle of mental and ethical traits. Integrity, good judgment, consistency under pressure, and discipline—all traits of good character—are all important to consider when you're building a world-changing team. But how can you know if a person has good character? It's not always as easy as you might think.

No matter how much due diligence we give during a hiring process, it can be easy to miss when it comes to character, particularly when a candidate's competence and capacity are high.

I once blew past red flags in an interview process with a hire I really wanted. I was infatuated with the idea of getting this man on staff, because he had come from a considerably larger place. I thought he could add value to our team, and frankly I was flattered that he wanted to leave his current employment to join us.

I went to his home for one of the interviews. When his wife came home from grocery shopping, she struggled past us several times, carrying bags of groceries. But he never made a move to help her. I wanted to help, but it seemed out of place, so I also sat still. Something clicked in my heart. *Something is wrong with this picture,* I thought. Still, I suggested that we would like to hire him as a director of ministry, and if that went well, he would move into the executive director of everything. Without a moment's consideration, he shot back that if he didn't come in as executive director, he would not come at all.

Looking back, I still can't believe I ignored the strong evidence that this man didn't have the kind of character that would have made someone a match for our needs. He was so gifted, and I had already made up my mind that we needed him, so I flew past the red flags and hired him. As it turned out, his was one of the shortest hires in our church's history. Within his first three months with us, our entire team knew that keeping him on staff would change our chemistry, calling, and DNA—and not for the better.

Your team members' character will determine the respect and consideration people give your story. When your story is the Gospel story, it's a matter of eternal life and death. That is why it is absolutely essential that you make sure that everyone who joins your team has the kind of character that should define your story.

Checkpoint #5—Clarity. If you want your team to change the world, you as leader must be absolutely clear on its purpose. Your team members may not know every step they will eventually take (you probably won't know that, either), but they need to understand where they are going. A single player who doesn't clearly know or agree with where the story is headed can derail the entire story, or mute its impact.

The Absalom syndrome refers to people on the team who are like King David's son, Prince Absalom. He did not buy into his father's vision for the nation and was forever lobbying for something different. He didn't see or appreciate David's vision. He couldn't persuade his father to change direction, so he sat at the city gate and called on people to abandon his father's vision. The Bible says he stole the hearts of the people away from the leader. Anyone who is not clear on and committed to a team's purpose and vision will eventually lead others away from that purpose.

Checkpoint #6—Chemistry. Many ingredients combine to make a winning team, and one of the most important is what is called "team chemistry." Good team chemistry can make the difference between an ordinary story and an outstanding one.

We can see the importance of team chemistry demonstrated in the world of competitive sports. A basketball team can possess five players with above-average talent, but that team will likely never go anywhere amazing unless the players are bonded together with a common spirit and purposefulness. On the other hand, being bonded together enables the players to work together harmoniously, willingly and unselfishly dovetailing their skills and talents for the common good.

Chemistry is the ability of the team members to get along with one another, to work together smoothly and unselfishly under leadership. It includes each member's recognition and acceptance of his or her specific roles. It also includes an element of mutual loyalty and empathy. It is the ability of the team members to anticipate one another's moves and to blend their efforts into one extraordinary story.

Make sure you don't bring someone into your story who obviously carries with him an awkwardness or unease. Most outstanding teams don't naturally have the chemistry they need to be successful, and you may need to work with your team members to develop and protect it.

Checkpoint #7—Coachability. Arrigo Sacchi, the master Italian soccer coach, said the most important qualities of the greatest players are humility and coachability. He defined coachability as a player's ability to take guidance from the coach and use it to constantly improve his performance.

Fact is, not everyone is coachable. Some people think they have no performance problems and that if there is an issue, "they," the people "out there," caused it. Attempts at coaching don't often produce positive results in a person who thinks that way. It's a lot like when one spouse drags the other to marriage counseling, hoping that the counselor's magic touch will "fix" the partner. That usually doesn't work out well, either, because one partner holds to a mind-set that doesn't allow him or her to reflect on his or her own behavior. It's also due to a lack of desire to change behavior or take personal responsibility for the relationship.

I have learned that forcing an uncoachable person into a coaching relationship isn't usually the best organizational solution for certain issues and individuals. I have tried to "coach" uncoachable people, even arranging for them to get free help from experts in their field, and been defensively refused, or met with a blank stare.

Only those who are coachable and committed to personal change can be in your winning story. Coachable people want to improve themselves and are willing to take responsibility for their own lives and step outside their comfort zones. They are open to hearing constructive criticism without being defensive and then synthesize the suggestions they receive with their own personal reflections.

Checkpoint #8—Cooperation. Effective teams are not just collections of people. Rather, they are a body that is greater than the sum of its parts. This means that team members must work together closely and make every effort to support and cooperate with each other.

Cooperation requires open communication, creative thinking, and team effort. When one team member is so dominant that others feel like they have to defend everything they say or prove a point to get cooperation, communication will shut down, creativity will die, and the team story will splinter. A successful team creates and sustains an environment that leads the team to achieve the goals of the leader.

That does not mean, however, that total agreement is required to make a team story successful, because the final say belongs to the leader. The leader ultimately assumes full responsibility for all decisions the group makes. When Henry Ford wanted his engine built, his engineers were in agreement that it could not be done. But Ford held fast to his unwavering courage and, in the end, it was done. He had the final say in the decision-making process because he knew it was his neck on the line. Cooperation is good as long as it does not lead to "groupthink," which can shut down the vision the leader knows is absolutely right.

After welcoming input from the team, a leader will sometimes need to revert to his or her sense of vision and assurance that a particular leading is of the Spirit.

Sometimes he or she will have to overrule the thoughts of the team, and then expect and receive full cooperation from team members in carrying out the ultimate decision.

In a Directional Leadership Team meeting, I announced a hire I was preparing to make. "Hold up," one of my valued team members said. "I thought to hire someone, we all have to agree."

"No," I responded. "I would *like* us all to agree. I value your input, I desire your opinion. But I am the one who is evaluated by our board. I am the one who answers for this decision. My vote outweighs all the rest of the votes put together. You give input, I make the call."

When an individual team member disagrees with the leader's vision and/or decisions, he or she has a choice: with a committed and clear spirit, cooperate with the decision the team leader has made, or leave the team. No matter how gifted a team member is, if he or she lacks the quality of willing, wholehearted cooperation, the team story will be undermined.

Checkpoint #9—Confidence. Contributors to a world-changing story have a sense of personal confidence, the kind of confidence that allows them to roll with the punches, handle disappointment, exercise patience, give credit to others, present with poise, unselfishly work for the good of the team, and more.

It is unlikely that your team will change the world

unless individual members are confident in who they are. When your team members lack that kind of confidence, problems such as envy and jealousy can come out in their ugliest forms.

Jesus was able to humbly take on the role of a servant because He was supremely aware of and confident in His own identity. John 13:3 (NIV) tells us where that powerful confidence originated: "Jesus knew that the Father had put all things under his power, and that he had come from God and was returning to God."

Jesus' relationship with His Father and His awareness of Himself and His purpose gave Him confidence. He knew where He came from, where He was going, and that His Father was empowering Him. For that reason, He didn't need to be grabby, self-protective, or maintain a posture.

Without similar confidence radiating from the same place, team members may struggle to live within the shadow of a great leader or an outstanding teammate. Wherever godly confidence thrives, changes can happen and new players can be added to the team without disruption to the story.

Acts 8 records that God used Philip to start a great revival in Samaria. But as soon as things were really popping, Peter and John showed up and essentially took over the preaching in the Samaritan villages, while God reassigned Philip to the desert. Did he pout? No! He was confident in who he was and in God's hand on his life. That enabled him to hear God's leading to speak to an Ethiopian man, which helped the Gospel story take another leap into a new nation.

On the other hand, God selected King Saul, Israel's first monarch, because he was "head and shoulders above everyone else" in key attributes. But when Saul's relationship with God lost its vitality, his confidence disappeared. He became jealous of David, even to the point of attempted murder.

Character assassinations, criticism, gossip—all of these ugly, destructive patterns flourish when team members lack confidence. But when I am confident that God is the supreme Author and that He is equipping me to do and be all that is His plan for me, I lose my envy and self-protectiveness. I cease monitoring how many lines I have in each chapter, and I know I won't be the main character in every chapter the team writes. I know I am part of the fantastic story, and it gives me great joy and fulfillment.

KNOWING WHEN TO LET GO

As hard as it may sometimes be, you must have the strength of character and leadership to develop effective team members and release ineffective members. Jesus made the call Himself: "He cuts off every branch in me that bears no fruit, while every branch that does bear fruit he prunes so that it will be even more fruitful" (John 15:2 NIV).

Jack Welch was chairman and CEO of General Electric between 1981 and 2001. During his tenure at GE, the company's value rose 4,000 percent. He said the number one responsibility of a leader is to continually evaluate and upgrade the team. Jesus did that all the time. He continually tested the twelve, and He sent the seventy out two by two to see how they did.

There is a price to pay at every level of writing a great, world-changing story, and some people will not be able or willing to go with you to the next level. Some people will reach their dream long before you do and be satisfied with what you are not. When that happens, thank them for their contributions and let them go. You cannot afford to diminish the story God has called you to write because you value a personal relationship or a person's feelings over wisdom and obedience.

I never want to lose anyone or break anyone's heart. But my job is to keep the vision God has given me alive. It would be wonderful if everyone could stay with us, but it's not always possible. Sometimes keeping the vision alive and well requires the loss of an individual, and that calls for courage and resolve from the leader.

LEADING WITH A GENEROUS SPIRIT

Greed is a huge enemy to any great story. When you are ambitious and focused on a big vision, it's easy to hold the resources God puts in your hand too closely to your chest. That includes your "human resources."

I don't envy anyone, and I don't want to ever hold anyone back from any opportunity. If another leader calls me and asks permission to talk to one of my key players about another job offer, I always give it. I want everyone to have the best opportunities possible, and I trust God. My job is to create a clear and compelling vision with opportunities to grow and actually change the world. If any "star player" leaves us, it is only because God had tapped him or her on the shoulder with directions to head for another place.

Proactively giving someone away is a little harder. A church I love and desire to prosper recently contacted me about dire needs in its worship program. Over a period of months, I gave them helpful advice, but then God clicked in on my heart and said, "You need to tell the pastor about Dan." I was reluctant to do that, because we had invested in this young man from his college days, and he was one of our key worship volunteers. I told God I had Dan in mind as worship leader for a campus we planned to start in the future.

God answered, "You are not using him to the max. He needs opportunities to grow and develop that you aren't currently giving him. They need someone now. If you don't have the faith to believe I will meet your need when it presents itself, you shouldn't start another campus because you aren't spiritually ready."

I recommended Dan, and now he is making great contributions to the church and growing in his faith.

This story illustrates the fact that God will meet our need when we have it. There is no room for greed and self-protectiveness as we write a great story.

MAKING CAMARADERIE A PRIORITY

Mutual experiences help build camaraderie and foster and protect your story. There is nothing like camaraderie based on shared experiences and memories. That's why it's important that you do all you can to give your team a sense of togetherness and teamwork.

This is one of the characteristics of the early church, which led to the explosion of the world's greatest story: "All the believers were together and had everything in common" (Acts 2:44 NIV).

You can accomplish that by praying together, serving together, and by socializing and having fun together. You can take a retreat away from the workplace together, or periodically have the team players share what they love and appreciate about each other. You can also ask team members to perform anonymous "random acts of kindness" for a different teammate each week.

FOSTERING PERSONAL GROWTH

Leadership is a lot like parenting. Occasionally I am asked, "In your structure, who is responsible for the growth of the team?" But that's not a one-person answer. As the leader, I am responsible for providing the team opportunities and input for growth, but the team members are all primarily responsible for their own spiritual growth.

So am I!

When I first graduated from college, I moved in with my sister, her husband, and their little daughter Rachel for a while. On my first day there, they said to me, "Here's the refrigerator and the pantry. Help yourself. If Rachel starves, it's our fault. If you starve, it's your fault."

That's the way it is with our team. Only infants need to be fed. If a team member does not keep pace with spiritual growth, the onus is on that person.

My niece Rachel is now grown with a baby of her own to feed. Most days, she and her husband feed themselves and their son. But every Monday night, all three of them have a standing invitation to come back home because Mom is cooking. Even though the invitation is open, it's up to the grown children to decide whether or not to accept it.

That is an apt illustration of how leaders should be fed. There should be a point when they "leave their house" and assume responsibility for feeding and growing themselves. The boss is no longer responsible for making sure they grow. But the boss/team leader should periodically issue an open invitation for everyone in the organization to come home and have a meal (training time) together. These team training times provide absolutely essential fellowship and information, but can't take the place of meals/growth on their own.

Leaders who want to carry their own weight must continue growing. They must develop the "households" or teams they lead and assume responsibility to feed and grow themselves. Model it, make the way for it, expect it.

Your leadership example is bigger and far more impactful than anything you will ever say. My personal assistant is consistently noticed for the above-and-beyond capability mixed with servant spirit she displays. Heather says she learned it long before she came to us by witnessing the behavior of the wealthy wife of her employer. This lady would see a need, and no matter how menial the work, without calling attention to herself, she would just go handle it. Heather says, "It seemed backwards to me. She was the owner. I was the employee. It so impressed me, it forever shaped who I am."

As you lead your team in its efforts to change the world, never forget that you are leading in an upside-down kingdom. The values of the story Jesus is writing through you are exactly the opposite of the values prized in the kingdom of this world. We serve the One who came not to be served, but to serve. He says anyone who wants to write a great story must be willing to take the position of least of all (see Mark 9:35). Write big and bold with the heart of a servant.

ACTION STEPS

1. Make a list of your team members, and commit yourself to regular seasons of prayer for them.

2. Communicate at least monthly with your team. Give team members feedback, encouragement, and correction.

3. Make an action plan for the things you personally need to address to grow as a leader.

11

{ Keeping Your Story Fresh }

Have you ever seen a movie or read a book that started out well but lost its way as the story progressed? Sure, it started out strong enough, but somewhere along the way, it turned weak. As you sit in your recliner watching the movie or reading the book, you lose interest and begin to wonder if the author even cared about the second half of the story. Reviewers would say the movie was over an hour before it ended.

That kind of thing can happen in your life, as well. As you write the story of your life, opportunities abound for it to lose its animation and momentum. Sadly, many people's once-promising stories turn mundane, leaving once-inspiring and joyful lives drab and, frankly, boring.

On the other hand, there are many examples of people whose lives, from beginning to end, consistently inspire us. In the news and entertainment world, there are Walter Cronkite and Oprah Winfrey. In sports, guys like Larry Bird and Troy Aikman have kept their stories strong and engaging well after their professional athletic careers ended. In politics, former United States president Jimmy Carter has become well known for his charitable endeavors after leaving the highest-profile position in the world. In the world of ministry, Billy Graham is one of the highest-profile spiritual leaders of all time. His story continues to grow more uplifting and inspiring in his ninetieth decade.

KEEPING YOUR STORY EXCITING

People who keep their stories alive and exciting—both to themselves and others—throughout their lifetimes do a few very important things differently than those who lose momentum. People are not simply born with a "karma" that propels them to ongoing success. On the contrary, the best authors, the ones who write with God, do some things those of us who want to keep our stories fresh and alive can emulate.

Here is a good list of those things:

1. *Identify and pursue S.M.A.R.T. goals.* In his book *Attitude Is Everything*, author Paul J. Myer says goals that fit this definition—SMART—are Specific, Measurable, Attainable, Relevant, and Timely:

Specific: While a general goal would be to read more, a specific and helpful goal would be to read at least two leadership books per month. A specific goal is not a "warm and fuzzy" that simply makes me feel good.

Because it has definition, I have a far greater chance of accomplishing it. A specific goal will usually answer the five "W" questions: what, why, who, where, and which.

Measurable: This answers questions like "How much?" "How many?" and "How will I know when it is accomplished?" To make your goals measurable, you need a system to track where you are and your target dates. Measuring progress keeps me motivated and moving.

Attainable: This usually answers the question "How exactly will I get there?" The goal must be large enough to stretch my vision, faith, and abilities, but it must be within the realm of possibility. For example, if I say, "I will become a runner," I've given voice to an attainable goal. But if I say, "I will run a marathon in one week," I've stated a goal that is both unrealistic and defeating.

Relevant: This applies to choosing goals that actually matter to my destination. For instance, I could set a goal of making five hundred paper airplanes between 9 a.m. and 7 p.m. every Thursday. That's specific, measurable, attainable—and even timely—but is it relevant to what God has called me to do? Relevant goals answer the questions: "Does this seem worthwhile?" "Is this the right time?" "Does this match our other efforts/needs?" and "Am I the right person?"

Timely: The goal is tied to a time period; there is a target date and checkpoints along the way. This is necessary to keep daily distractions from overtaking our goals. It helps us to focus on our work by regularly asking the question, "By when?"

Identifying S.M.A.R.T. goals motivates and inspires me. It fuels my desire to grow and develop skills and resources necessary to bring my goals to pass. Almost anything can be accomplished when I set goals with God and wisely plan my life to reach them. I grow to the size of the goals I set.

2. Be decisive and make informed decisions. Every spring, high school and college graduates share their dreams and visions of what their future is going to look like. Sad to say, most of them will never reach the future they describe. It won't be because they weren't capable or because they lacked the knowledge or resources to make it happen. Almost 100 percent of the time, their failure to reach the life of their dreams is directly attributable to one reason: *they never took action.*

There is a huge difference between acquiring knowledge and growing. Growth happens when you purposely take action. People who keep it fresh learn by seeking wise counsel. Proverbs 11:14 (NASB) directs, "Where there is no guidance the people fall, but in abundance of counselors there is victory." Getting good counsel is particularly important when our emotions are high. Sometimes we do foolish things simply because of temporary emotions. Emotional decisions often lead us astray when we are trying to write a great story line. Successful and inspiring people, on the other hand, proactively get the best information they can, and then they actually take action based on what they have learned. Everything is useless without action. It's as simple as that. "Freshness" flows from wise, decisive action.

3. Overcome disappointment. Do you remember your childhood dreams? Maybe you thought you would be a professional athlete, a famous actress, or an astronaut. Or maybe your dreams were more simple and serious. Maybe you dreamed your parents would get back together or that you wouldn't have to move to a new town for your senior year.

What happens when those dreams go unfulfilled? Unfortunately, for most of us, once reality taints our dreams and a few of them die, we quit allowing ourselves the joy of dreaming big. The older we get, the more crushing disappointment can become, because our adult dreams carry so much weight.

When disappointment comes, we often feel empty and uncertain and begin wrestling with our purpose and calling. This is especially painful when we have tied our worth and significance to how something turns out. But people who stay fresh and inspiring do not let disappointment define them.

In July 2012, Ernie Els won the British Open in a surprise victory. Adam Scott, the expected champion, bogeyed his last four holes, three shots over on the last two holes. Announcers said Scott had "one hand on the cup," but he still lost it. A sportscaster asked Els, the older and more experienced player, "What did you say to Adam after his agonizing defeat?"

Els replied, "I told him to not linger over this loss too long. I did it in the past, and it nearly wrecked my career. You will have other opportunities to win. Do not beat yourself up too badly. You have to move on."

Excellent advice.

You are not the sum total of your wins and losses. Don't let disappointment and perceived failure crush you. Own whatever responsibility you need to, and learn from it. Cry and grieve and work through your emotions. Then remind yourself of who you are in Christ and move on. You are still extraordinarily gifted and still called. Don't let momentary disappointment keep you from all the adventure you were meant to live.

4. Continue to risk and sacrifice. I have heard married couples speak nostalgically and wistfully about the early days of their marriages, when they "didn't have two cents to rub together." But when they reached a point in their life together when they no longer *had* to sacrifice and take risks together, they stopped being challenged, and their love lost some of its sparkle. That happens in individual life stories, too. Sometimes we enjoy enough success early on that we actually don't need to do anything risky or sacrificial to maintain. . .and so we don't. Then the zest for living withers away. When we aren't excited about our stories, no one else gets much from them, either.

People who keep it fresh continually make new choices, head new directions, and lay it on the line. Patty and I actively practice that, and it keeps us close to each other, close to God, and on our knees.

The most recent large risk we took was committing a year of our salary over three years to our "Only God" campaign. We live by the principle of radical generosity beyond our tithes, but this was the second time we had given a year's salary. The first time, our children were smaller and had fewer needs, so the sacrifices involved just Patty and me. This time around, however, we had two kids in college and two still at home.

When we first discussed this sacrifice, we asked ourselves, "How many times can we do this crazy stuff?" But we took the leap, made the pledge, and began altering our lifestyle so we could make the necessary sacrifices. Despite our best efforts, we fell behind in our giving. But within the first six months of our new commitment, we received a letter from a publisher asking us to write this book. We plan to give any money we get from the book to God to fund His dream. Right at the time we need it, He comes through in amazing ways.

Do you ever wish you were more spiritual? More like

John Wesley? Me too. Wesley is reported to have regularly prayed seven hours a day. I can wish I was more like John Wesley all I want, but I'm just not that guy. But when I actually take a risk and make sacrifices for God's kingdom, I am drawn to Him like a child to its mother.

Every year I commit to something only God can accomplish through me. This motivates me to pray without ceasing because it makes me utterly aware of my dependence on Him. We are *all* dependent on God. It's just that some of us are not as aware that we are, because our lives are too easy, too comfortable, and too risk-free.

I try to consciously put myself in positions to heighten my awareness that I am done if God doesn't come through for me. Talk about risk! Talk about freshness and momentum in my story! I feel like I am living a walking and talking chapter of the Acts of the Apostles!

5. Avoid the perfectionism trap. High achievers who want to change their world understand that excellence is necessary for a great story. That is why they set high standards for themselves and why their passion for excellence drives them to run the extra mile.

But what happens when we aim beyond excellence to perfection? First of all, we have a hard time getting started because conditions are never perfect. When we miss the impossible standards of perfection, we become disgruntled and discouraged with ourselves and with others.

This causes major delays, inefficiency, stress overload, and less-than-desired results. Perfectionism takes the joy and energy out of our stories.

Life rarely rewards perfectionism but almost always rewards people who get things done. People who write the great stories focus on excellence and keep their energy and freshness alive by getting things done.

6. *Spend time with the right people.* There are people who bring joy when they *enter* the room, and there are people who bring joy when they *leave*. There are people who add energy to life when they arrive, and there are people who add energy when they depart. Those whose stories are fresh and invigorating deliberately spend the bulk of their time with the right people.

It is very easy for compassionate world changers to blunt their impact on the world they love by spending too much time with unhealthy and draining people. Pastor and author Gordon MacDonald wrote about VDPs—Very Draining People. These are folks who drain our energy rather than refuel us. You cannot completely avoid VDPs, but you can help yourself develop a positive and productive story by choosing to limit your exposure to and interaction with them.

You are largely the result of the people with whom you spend your time. Negative people will negatively affect you, but positive people will help you expand your story and make you more capable and knowledgeable than you could have been without them.

The Billy Graham Association and its decades-long story, written through the crusades and the worldwide evangelism, came about because a few high-quality friends (Billy Graham, Cliff Barrows, George Beverly Shea, Grady Wilson, T. W. Wilson) committed themselves to friendships based on integrity and productivity and shaped each other over the years. Wherever you find greatness, you'll find stories like this one.

Great people don't grow in isolation. Whenever you find one great person writing an amazing story, you will find others nearby. That's why great people have great friends. Most often, they didn't make those friends *after* they became great; they wrote parts of their story of greatness with their friends nearby. Significant people make their primary associations with people who are like-minded, focused, and supportive. They reach out to connected, influential individuals who complement their dreams and goals and nudge them on to greatness.

7. *Live a life of intentional influence.* Almost nothing extraordinarily wonderful happens by accident. I have realized how true this is in many areas, but for the longest time, I totally overlooked it in the area of influence. I just assumed that my responsibility was to live well, and along the way God would bring into my path people I could naturally influence. Of course, we do naturally influence people to some degree, but not to the exciting

level we can when we do it with *intentionality.*

God opened my eyes to this principle through a friendship with a successful businessman who one day asked me, "Why has God blessed me so much?" I told him God had blessed him with his resources so he could be a blessing to others. I challenged him with the thought, "Don't die with a million dollars in the bank. You need to be intentional. Use it to be a blessing and change the world."

A few years later, this man came back to me with a word of wisdom. He basically said, "Dwight, you have more influence than you realize. Be more intentional with it. Use it to change the world." God took the words I had spoken to this man and returned them to me, also telling me, "You don't have a million dollars, but you have a million dollars' worth of influence. Don't die with it in the bank, or you don't get any credit."

True leadership is intentional influence—willful, planned, on purpose. Great leaders keep their stories fresh by persuading, empowering, inspiring, encouraging, and stimulating the right people—not by accident, but on purpose. You have great influence. When you intentionally use it, it will enhance your story.

8. Do what is right and needed, not what is comfortable or exciting. The first stages of anything that ends up great are often unspectacular. For example, before Olympic athletes can hear the applause of the crowd, they must spend many grueling hours alone, sweating, and in pain, denying themselves what "everyone else" enjoys. Many a gifted athlete who had the innate potential has never made it to Olympic glory, simply because he or she ran to what was exciting or comfortable *now* instead of what would pay the biggest dividend in the future.

The authors with ever-fresh story lines have a willingness to go outside their comfort zones. They are willing to plod through something they need to do now *if* it is necessary for satisfaction in the long run. They commit to what is right and needed instead of what feels comfortable and is "good enough."

These attitudes make a world of difference in achieving goals and tangible success. That is true even more so in the eternal realm of relationships. Early in my marriage, a leadership couple in the church—old enough to be our parents—became deeply involved in our family life. They loved Patty and me and our children, along with our entire extended family, and we loved them back. We spent many ordinary days and holidays with them. After quite a few years, our relationship with this couple came to a difficult place over the church's relocation project. The couple eventually left our church, and the friendship ended. It was a very painful parting to us and possibly to them as well. We went our separate ways and, even in our small community, rarely saw them or heard anything about them—until the day we heard that the wife had terminal cancer. Our hearts were broken, and I was at a total loss as to what to do. I wanted to go see her, but I was afraid. Because we had parted painfully, I envisioned the visit going badly. They were friends with many of our former board members, and I pictured me showing up in the hospital room, facing a hostile group of people, all thinking, *What are you doing here? Don't you know we are angry with you? We don't want you here.*

In spite of my fears, I decided to take a risk and go to see her. Patty went with me, and when we walked into the room, only our dear sick friend and her daughter were there. I will never forget her first words:

"I knew you would come."

I wonder who has waited for me to enter their situation, but I never showed up because doing so might have felt awkward or uncomfortable. I wonder what other decisions I have avoided making because I allowed fear to take hold of me.

People whose stories burst with life all the way through do what is right and what is needed consistently, no matter how it feels.

9. Develop balance and rhythm in life. Somewhere along the way, our culture came to accept a misguided stereotype of a successful individual—the driven workaholic. While living life that way may lead to financial reward, it won't yield true success and significance. A life without rhythm and balance makes for a lousy story.

A meaningful, satisfying life is composed of several

dimensions, and we all need to learn to strike a balance between them. No one can keep their lives balanced in every single area on every single day. There are times when, because of the demands of the day, we must tend to the absolute essentials and temporarily put certain areas of life on hold. For example, I know my physical health is important, and I try to maintain a schedule of physical exercise. But there are days when balance demands that I forgo the exercise I had planned and give that time to other concerns, such as my children.

This is one reason it's so important to set priorities. As a matter of principle, after my relationship with Christ, my relationship with my family is my next priority.

When you let your work life (or social life, family life, etc.) consume you, and you focus all your energy on that one area, it's extremely easy to lose your balance and write an uneven story. Drive and focus are important, but if you're going to get things right, you need to balance the various dimensions of your life. Neglecting one dimension of life for another leads to long-term frustration and stress for you and for those who are important to you.

Balance is best achieved when we find a rhythm for life. God laid that pattern for us when He Himself rested after six days of work and set aside every seventh day for us to do the same. In fact, I believe that a fresh story is far more about rhythm than balance. Some helpful things I have learned for my own healthy rhythm are:

- Instead of trying to maintain a rigid balance, I put purpose and passion into every moment. That way, whether I am shooting hoops with my son, working on a household project with Patty, or putting in long hours at a new multisite, I find fulfillment and joy.

- Rather than thinking of things a day at a time, I look at weeks and months. During pressurized weeks, given days may be imbalanced; or during periods of relaxation, work may take a back burner. Overall, though, I have a healthy balance in my life. Figure out which elements need to be in your life and what is a reasonable amount of time, during the course of a week or a month, to devote to each.

- Build up a pocketful of "change" at work and at home. When the family needs you, cheerfully give all you have. When the job needs you, go above and beyond. That will give you some wiggle room when you aren't able to come through the way you would like.

- Build a rhythm with your family for renewal and refreshment. Lunchtime and the afternoon on Fridays are set aside for time with Patty. It would practically take a state emergency to interrupt that time. We both anticipate it and can hold on through stressful moments, because we know our time is coming. Regular dates with all your family members are rhythms worth establishing. Everyone will anticipate the time and draw strength from the memory afterward.

- Days off, downtime, and vacation are nonnegotiable. First Kings 19 tells us that the prophet Elijah, one of God's mightiest men, lost the exuberance in his story because of exhaustion but he got it back when he rested. Jesus Himself often withdrew from the crowds and went to solitary mountains to retreat and revive.

- A personal Sabbath is the only way to keep the spirit fresh. If you are a deeply involved church leader, it's likely that Sunday can't be that time of relaxation for you. Find another time to regularly turn off the engine and refuel.

10. *Focus on small, consistent improvements, and keep*

track of their progress. Henry Ford, a man whose story was big enough to change the world, said, "Nothing is particularly hard if you divide it into small pieces." When the size of a task is intimidating, taking the first small step and succeeding is motivational and rewarding. It gets you excited and hopeful about your life, and others feel the same.

Do you think it's important to balance your bank account from time to time? Of course it is! You need to monitor fees, withdrawals, and deposits so you can know where you are financially and so you can avoid accidentally depleting your account. You can't control what you don't properly track and measure. People whose stories thrill and motivate step back and assess their progress regularly. They track themselves against their goals and clearly know what needs to be done to excel and accelerate.

11. Be supportive of others. Great authors know their story isn't the only good one being written, so they generously offer others encouragement, support, and resources. They are optimistic and devoid of jealousy and envy. They believe there is all the room in the world for everyone to be as great as they want to be. They don't waste time worrying about who is doing what, and they applaud the successes of others.

Fresh people know that most folks are a mix of good and bad, strength and weakness. They understand that we all get to choose what we focus on in others. If you want improvement, focusing on the good in people is a useful choice that also makes life easier for you and your world and relationships more pleasant and positive.

When you choose to focus on the good in others, it becomes easier to love and serve them. By serving other people, by adding value to their lives, you not only make their lives better, but over time you tend to get back what you have given. The people you support will themselves be more inclined to help others. That is how you can create an upward spiral of positive change that grows and becomes stronger.

12. Connect your beliefs to your behavior. A double life is exhausting. We can easily become wearied when we say one thing and live another. King David had the platform to observe and reflect on both refreshing lives and draining lives. He wrote that consistently rejecting what is evil and holding to all that is good is the secret to a fresh and fruitful story:

> *Happy are those who don't listen to the*
> *wicked, who don't go where sinners go,*
> *who don't do what evil people do.*
> *They love the LORD's teachings,*
> *and they think about those teachings day*
> *and night.*
> *They are strong, like a tree planted by a river.*

The tree produces fruit in season, and its leaves don't die.

Everything they do will succeed.

PSALM 1:1–3 NCV

ACTION STEPS

1. Reflect over how your life has gone the past year. Evaluate your story. Is it building in strength or waning?

2. Look ahead to the next year. What can you build into your life so that the fresh wind of God's Spirit can bring new life to your story?

12

{ Hungry for More }

To those who follow professional golf, John Daly is a conundrum. He is seen as having all the potential in the world and has actually won a few major championships. But instead of capitalizing on his wins and moving in among the ranks of the best of the best to play the game, he lost his tour card and became as well known for his antics on and off the course as for his golf game. A charming and charismatic guy golf fans love, Daly is often described as a player who has the goods to be a major winner but lacks the hunger and passion to actually make it happen.

Every championship arena in life requires hunger and passion. In every area, the greatest stories catch the imagination and fire the future, leaving the reader hungry for more. Writing a great story whets the appetites of the participants for *more* of your story. Changing your story paves the way for greater and greater opportunities. But to inspire hunger in others, you have to live hungry for more yourself.

When we start writing a bigger and better story, we have dreams and goals that may seem audacious or even unreachable to us at the time. As we take advantage of the "only God" moments He gives us, we grow ourselves and change our worlds. We meet our current goals, and new opportunities come as a result. At that point, we get to make another life-altering choice: Will we stay hungry and keep moving forward, or will we be content with simply doing more than the average?

A HUNGRY KIND OF FAITH

Patty and I named our first son after a Bible hero who got it right. Caleb was Joshua's peer and coleader, one of only two people from the entire nation of Israel who fully believed God.

Caleb was one of the twelve spies Moses sent in to check out the land God was giving them. Ten of the spies saw giants and other problems in the Promised Land as bigger than the opportunity. But two of them, Caleb and Joshua, were hungry for all God had promised. These two men didn't ignore the challenges they would face, but they were convinced they were more than able to meet them.

After the rest of the entire unbelieving generation died in the desert, Joshua and Caleb led the charge of a new generation into Canaan. Caleb wasn't satisfied to have just made it there so he could enjoy the spoils available to every Israelite. He was eighty-five at the time, and though he was the eldest in the nation, he didn't make a graceful exit to a rocking chair. Joshua 14 tells us that Caleb was not one to live off the past. Sure, he remembered how God had demonstrated His faithfulness in the past, but time had not dimmed his vision or filled his hunger. He did not ask for any easy place where he could spend his remaining years in peace and quiet. He saw the place where he currently stood not as a deserved reward, but as an opportunity to exercise faith and claim new victories.

So Caleb asked for the most difficult place of all, a mountainous area where giants were entrenched and where the fierce Anakim guarded the cities. He was hungry for new victories. He thanked God for his vigor and strength, but he didn't depend on these things. He confessed his need for God's help and demonstrated a faith firmly grounded on God's promises.

Caleb's life demonstrated the kind of hunger that fulfills us and attracts others to our story. This hungry faith was characteristic of Caleb's entire life. His faith never wavered. Numbers 13 and 14 report that Caleb and Joshua believed they were big enough for *anything* God commanded. As the British evangelist/author Alan Redpath said, "The majority had great giants but a little God. Caleb [and Joshua] had a great God and little giants."

Through all forty years of wandering in the wilderness, Caleb kept the faith. He never doubted that God would fulfill His promise that they would enter the land. When the people rebelled against Moses, Caleb did not. Never was he among those who grumbled, never did he want to return to the strange comfort of slavery in Egypt, and never did he participate in disobedience and idolatry.

Caleb had a strength that never weakened. He testified that he was as strong at age eighty-five as he had been when Moses sent him into Canaan as a spy forty-five years earlier. I am certain he meant physical strength, because he specifically mentioned that he was strong "for war." But the same thing could clearly be said of his spiritual and emotional strength. Science, medicine, and religion all agree that our faith and future outlook really have the lion's share in determining our health. Caleb was an example of the fact that living with passion and hunger equips us to stay strong and to live long and well.

Because of all of this, Caleb's victory was complete and his story was incredible. Joshua 15 tells us Caleb succeeded in driving the Canaanites out of his territory, among them the three giant sons of Anak. These were the same giants the ten spies had said Israel could not defeat. None of the tribes was able to clear the Canaanites from their territories. Caleb was the only one who succeeded in expelling the enemy from his territory. The man who followed the Lord in everything, with a voracious hunger for more than the norm, was the only man who gained complete victory.

HUNGERING FOR "MORE"

When I became a pastor, churches in my denomination that grew to 200 to 250 in average attendance were considered large. If a pastor led a successful building program and had a nice building, had an average of a few hundred in attendance, met the missions budget, paid the assessments, and led people to the Lord along the way, he or she was an undisputed success.

Early on, my professional goals had been fairly simple: do the things listed above, love God and people, see lives changed, have the people in my church appreciate me, and have my peers in ministry acknowledge me. By God's grace, and through the amazing Christ followers in the Sugarcreek church, I accomplished those goals during my first years of ministry.

I had a brief period of feeling pleased and grateful for my accomplishments, but then a restlessness gripped my soul. God told me directly and unmistakably, "If you do not do another thing, you will have succeeded in man's eyes. But make no mistake—you will have failed in Mine." This conversation with the Lord awakened within me a new hunger to keep moving on and never be satisfied with anything less than all He wants for me. There's always a next level to reach, always a new place to go.

The sense that my definition of success must be different than what the eyes can see has never left me. Regardless of what I have accomplished, the only testimony that matters to me is that I be able to say, as Jesus did, "I have brought you glory on earth by finishing the work you gave me to do" (John 17:4 NIV). God keeps me hungry for that by regularly bringing challenging people and ideas into my life. Frankly, I am overwhelmed with what we are doing right now. My biggest challenge is to maintain a vibrant walk with God and to be faithful to everything He is calling me to in the moment.

When I first became a pastor, I thought I was going to change the world by doing something great for God in Sugarcreek, and that God would use that success to give me greater influence in my denomination. But it hasn't gone that way. I say without hurt or disappointment that I never gained significant influence in my denomination.

I love the church, and I always will. I never intended to do anything except spend my life serving as a denominational pastor. But there came a time when what God saw as necessary and obedient for me and NewPointe did not mesh with our denomination's vision. We reluctantly came to the conclusion that we would need to maintain a fraternal relationship of love and encouragement with our denomination but sever our official ties. I still love the church of my birth, and I would do anything to further one of its pastors or congregations.

Because our weaknesses are so often lifetime battles, my fear of being misunderstood and my desire to please others gave me some difficult days. However, when you believe with all your heart that God is good and great, and that He can be fully trusted, He grows your character. You can obey and let the chips fall where they may, even when doing so is painful or frightening. My hunger for all God has for me to be and do, and my vital daily connection with Him, carried NewPointe and me through with unity and strength. We were poised for action, and growth accelerated.

Our hunger for more is very specific. We are hungry to win the I-77 Corridor in Ohio. It is our desire to go from the Ohio River (Marietta) to the lake (Lake Erie in Cleveland) and have life-changing impact on those cities and people. Our vision is to reach northeast Ohio through a threefold strategy:

> 1. Believing that the local church living and teaching the truth of Jesus Christ is the hope of the world, we want to launch multisites to strategically reach the people of specific cities or towns. The goal is to provide a safe place where they can hear a life-changing message in the language of today.

> 2. We will reach out to the marketplace/business world of our targeted communities. I believe most businesspeople have enjoyed a certain level of success, only to find out that it does not completely satisfy their hunger for more. All people

ultimately long for significance. If you don't understand that significance is more important than success, you set yourself up for disappointment and even destruction of the very things you have said are the most important to you—such as marriage, family, and character. We want to lead businesspeople toward character development and growth and sustain and support them as they face the challenges of doing business and leading their communities to positive change.

3. We will reach students and help them shape their worlds at the best possible time in their lives. It has been said that our children are getting older at a younger age than ever before. We desire to come alongside our schools to help train and develop students in principles and values that equip them for significance and success.

We are also hungry to make a major impact for God through missions, targeting the Middle East particularly, and to equip and empower national leaders to change their worlds. We believe God is still unveiling His vision. We have found that every time God unfolds a little more of that vision, it causes our faith to stretch, which leads us to more and more "only God" moments.

A STILL-DEEPER COMMITMENT

These are massive goals, big statements of faith. They express a huge hunger. When I first shared our vision with my consultant friend Bruce, he said, "Your dream is bigger than NewPointe. You are going to have to have help." At that moment I had second thoughts. I wasn't sure I wanted to go there. I wasn't feeling underchallenged as it was, and the thought of extending my reach one more time caused me to slow down, evaluate, and commit again to finishing all God calls me to do.

Starbucks cups occasionally bear some wisdom, and I found this quote (by Anne Morris, identified as a Starbucks customer from New York City) on one of them to be absolutely dead on: "The irony of commitment is that it's deeply liberating. . . . The act frees you from the tyranny of your internal critic, from the fear that likes to dress itself up and parade around as rational hesitation. To commit is to remove your head as the barrier to your life."

When I recommitted myself to following God's vision, my emotions cleared and my next steps became obvious.

First, I understood that no one can go to the next level in pursuing a dream without going to the next level in his or her relationship with God. I had to start there. God showed me, on mental index cards, what that meant. The first card told me to commit to and arrange my schedule to spend more focused time with Patty and our children. I had to build our home life even stronger and deeper than it had been. The second card addressed my thought life. Understand, I had long been cooperating with God on purity in my thought life. I never watched movies, looked at magazines, or opened websites that would compromise my devotion to Patty or give me opportunities to sin. I was very careful to not allow myself to have personal interactions that could put wrong thoughts into my mind. But God targeted a little leak Satan sometimes used to drop in wrong images: "No more surfing TV channels during commercials." Sounds small, but God impressed on me that the higher I went in my dreams with Him and His vision for me, the more sensitive I had to be to potential problem areas, and the more exacting my obedience needed to become.

If God is going to use you for great things, you must be greatly surrendered to Him. As stated earlier, "If you want God to do to something He has never done before, He's going to ask you to do something you have never done before." That is so true. You must meet God's hunger for you to fulfill everything He dreamed in you when He created you in your mother's womb with your own great hunger and obedience.

Second, God called me to an intimate time of developing my relationship with Him. He challenged me to spend one hundred hours in prayer over a three-month period. During that time, I was impressed to simply read the book of Genesis and ask God to speak to my heart.

As He spoke to me, I didn't try to evaluate what seemed wise and what seemed crazy, and I didn't try to write the ideas in any journalistic form to share. I simply recorded what God brought to my attention every day during those times of prayer and waiting on Him. God spoke to me so clearly that I could hardly wait for my times alone with Him. I truly hungered and thirsted for all He could give me.

God's messages to me came with great personal clarity. I am sure that the full meaning of what He said to me will be unfolding for the rest of my life. But patterns emerged in what He was speaking to me through His Word, especially through the stories of other men who hungered for more, like Abraham and Joseph. My eyes well up with tears and my heart fills with anticipation as I reread things God spoke to me. Simple sentences, weighty with meaning, for my life:

> *I will bless you and make you a blessing.*
> *Always honor Me—quickly. Do not fear, I*
> *am your shield and I myself will be your re-*
> *ward. Nothing is too hard for Me. Influence*
> *is a very fragile thing. Guard it. I know*
> *the motives of men's hearts. I will be faith-*
> *ful to you. People will notice when I am on*
> *your side. They will know that you have My*
> *favor, but don't take advantage of it. The*
> *power of walking faithfully with Me over*

*a long period of time is unfathomable. God
will always make a way. The people you
surround yourself with are very important.
You can shrug off the very rights God has
given you, if you give into your appetites.
There will always be famines—they reveal
who you really are and where you depend
on for help. Blessings always follow obedience. Birthright and blessings are huge in
the family of God. Don't lose either one of
them. I will birth something bigger through
you than you can imagine. If I am obedient,
God will stay with me and protect me until
He has done everything He has promised.
Sin will never stay hidden. Vision and
dreams can make people jealous. Be careful
of the pace at which you lead. You need to
increase your accountability.*

As God spoke through His Word and I responded,
my hunger for more of Him kept growing, and He
worked in areas of need in my life. As I read Genesis
32, God's voice asked me the same question He asked
Jacob: "What is your name?" In honesty and brokenness,
I owned that my name was "Pleaser."

When Jacob wrestled with God and owned what his
name had been, God responded in grace and power, giving him a new name, a name that would foreshadow the

rest of his life. God did that for me, too. When I owned that I was "Pleaser," overeager to gain approval and blessing from people, my Father gave me a new name. He told me, "From now on you will be 'Courageous.'" Those words poured power into me. Since that moment, I have stood taller and walked stronger. I truly am a new man with a new name, and I find great satisfaction and joy in living up to the name my Father gave me.

The third thing God did was give me some specific steps to take. One step was to do as Joseph did in the days of plenty: store up food to share with people in need. I understood that God was telling me to prepare for leadership training, conferences, workshops, and books. I was to put the food He fed me in a fashion to feed others. Shortly after that, I received a surprise invitation to write this book.

We began LEADER'S EDGE to train business leaders, are developing leadership forums on several levels ourselves, and cooperating with others. Another step was to follow up on several names God brought to my mind and explore partnerships for reaching our goals. One of the most significant challenges was to make a list of thirty businesspeople, many I didn't even know, and begin praying daily for them that God would fulfill His purpose in their lives.

Within a month of daily prayer for these thirty businesspeople, I received an e-mail from one of them, a successful and well-known leader in our area. The e-mail said, "Praying for you and NewPointe as you touch the world." What an encouragement! So, when God upped the ante on me and said it was time for me to move from prayer alone to making contact with these people, I went for the most straightforward businessman in the area and asked for a breakfast appointment. My fear reared its head again. I was scared to death. My tongue and throat were cottony as I pictured this man thinking I was arrogant and pushy. God spoke to me again. "Hey, Courageous," He said, "I am not depending on you to succeed. I am depending on you to be obedient. My responsibility is to make the ball hit the bat. You just have to step up to the plate and swing." Immediately, I felt different. The pressure was off. I knew I had no other responsibility but to obey God and to be as gracious and honest with this man as I could.

When I met with this leader, I told him I wanted to be transparent with him, share my passion with him, and invite him to consider participation, but I didn't want him to feel pressured or to think I was arrogant. This businessman smiled and answered, "I don't think that. How do you think I got where I am? You are just giving me an opportunity to be part of something. That's exactly what I do. I share and invite."

As I poured out my heart to this wise and generous man, I said, "I am not trying to get you to come to NewPointe—what I am talking about is bigger than a church. I don't want you to give me any money you are giving to your local church. If you are giving the maximum amount of money right now you can give anywhere, I do not want a penny of it redesignated to this cause. Truly, we need your prayers more than money, and we don't want any money that is already going into the kingdom of God."

He looked straight back at me and said, "I am interested. I am *very* interested. I have made more money in the last three years than in all of my previous years of business. I get hundreds of letters a year asking me for money to support a cause, and I throw them all away. If a person wants me to believe in their passion, but they can't meet with me face-to-face to share it, I figure it can't be that important."

That leadership lesson was worth more to me than the money this man donated.

God keeps showing me the same truth He has shown so many leaders throughout time. When I obey and do what I can do, God starts sending me people to fill in the gaps and do what I cannot do.

Any day now, God will make sure you meet just the person you need. The timing and resources will be so tailor-made that you will be in awe of how perfectly God worked it out. Gifted and able people, some you don't even know yet, are getting ready, waiting in the wings, to help you at just the right time in exactly the right way. Never give up because you don't know how it's going to happen or who will help you. Trust God for what you need when you need it. As the psalmist wrote, "Commit your way to the LORD! Trust him! He will act" (Ps. 37:5 CEB).

The thirty people I pray for daily are remarkable folks with skills, abilities, resources, and wisdom I do not possess. Every one of them has been moved to tears as we talked together. They have been watching the story, reading the chapters, hungering for more in our lives and in their own. One man said to me, "I have built a successful business, but am still yearning for something. I don't feel like I have done anything significant, anything that truly matters, with my life yet. Thank you for this opportunity."

Another man who is in his seventh decade of life has known remarkable success and owns many businesses in our area. After he agreed to an appointment with me, I went to our meeting with a tremendous amount of respect, maybe even a little awe, because of who he was. I told him what we were about, and a little apologetically made my "ask." His answer shook me to my core: "Dwight, I have watched you from a distance, and the consistency of your story and drive has spoken to me. You have earned the right to ask anything of me."

I couldn't keep the tears from my eyes. I had to ask his forgiveness because I had let my fear keep me from the conversation we both had needed to have for years.

STAY HUNGRY!
Anyone who wants to change the world and experience God—and the things only He can do—must unwaveringly

pursue the full vision He has shown them. Robert Quinn, author of *Deep Change*, says, "Acting on a vision that exceeds our resources is a test of our vision, faith, and integrity. When present resources determine the future, we have a plan, not a vision. A vision leads toward a plan that exceeds present resources."

As I've said before, whenever we get God's vision and actively pursue it, the people and resources start to show up. When we have enough faith to believe God and follow His direction, and the belief that we can actually do it, it sends the powerful message that who we are and what we are doing is worth someone else's investment. However, more than talk is needed. Our actions deliver a message mere words cannot.

When you stay hungry and obedient, God will do more than you can ask or imagine. You will be overwhelmed with the way He blesses you and multiplies your efforts. But you will need to always remember that it is Him doing it. James tells us that God opposes the proud. Doesn't that jolt you just a little? If I allow myself to become proud of what I am accomplishing and think it is all about me, God will actually start working against me.

Humility and hunger are a power-packed combination. When you are hungry for all God wants to accomplish through you, when you are willing to listen and obey and make whatever sacrifices are required, when you stay humble and give God all the glory, then there is nothing He cannot do in you or through you. And you will find others eager to join you and help you write new pages in a story the world needs.

ACTION STEPS

1. Write your personal definition of success. Commit it to memory.

2. Is there a step up in your relationship with God you know you must make before He will do something greater in your life? If so, what is it and what will you do about it?

3. What do you desire your legacy to be?

13

{ The Last Page }

The apostle Paul's last page is an impressive one. Sensing that the end is near, he writes to his close friend and spiritual son Timothy: "I have fought the good fight, I have finished the race, I have kept the faith. Now, a crown is being held for me—a crown for being right with God. The Lord, the judge who judges rightly, will give the crown to me on that day—not only to me but to all those who have waited with love for him to come again" (2 Tim. 4:7–8 NCV).

Paul's final comments to Timothy make it clear that the last page of his life was the best of them all. That's not nearly as common as you might think. Sadly, not every outstanding leader finishes well. In a study of more than 1,500 Christian leaders and Christ followers throughout history, Dr. J. Robert Clinton, Fuller Theological Seminary professor, made a startling discovery: Only one in three leaders finished strong. Two-thirds of these once-admired leaders stumbled before their last page, and their stories ended in disappointment and sometimes tragedy.

I have personally witnessed the waves of pain and disillusionment rolling like tides over families, churches, communities, and even entire nations when a leader quits writing a pure story line. After personally observing the loss suffered because of a moral failure in a family she knew, my daughter spoke to me hoarsely through tears, "Dad, don't you *ever* betray Mom. And if you ever do anything wrong, don't make it worse by lying about it."

Seeing and hearing about the pain, as well as the lost legacies bad decisions can cause, has powerfully impacted me. That's one of the reasons my desire to finish well figures prominently in every professional, ministry, and personal decision I have made for years. You ask, "Even small decisions?"

TIMES OF TESTING

I believe God allows each of us to face tests of our character and obedience, and each one of them builds upon the next. We can't keep writing great stories if we don't pass the tests.

In a three-month span almost two decades ago, I faced three challenges to my obedience, all of them related to one another. It is now absolutely clear to me that a failure to pass any one of these tests would have forever changed my story. I didn't ace any of the tests—I was afraid and dragged my feet—but God was patient with me, and I eventually passed.

The first was the test of relationships. Jesus made a

seemingly harsh statement to His disciples, "Unless you hate your mother and father, you can't follow Me." For me, Christ's command that no relationship can take precedence over obedience to Him didn't actually involve my family but a very close relationship to the family.

One of our staff members was also a friend I loved dearly. He was a good man, and I desperately wanted him to succeed. Over time, his leadership did not keep up with the pace of the church. Trying to find a fix for the problem and still retain this friend on staff, I received management advice and consulted with church leadership experts.

Every direction I went told me that we had come to the end of the road and that, for the good of all involved, I needed to release this good man to serve somewhere else. It was an agonizing decision for me. I knew I would be misunderstood, and to this day being misunderstood remains one of my biggest fears and pains. But God asked me, "Are you willing to lay your relationships on the line to do what I tell you?"

That's not the last time God has asked me that question, but passing that test the first time gave me strength and confidence that God would be with me through anything He required me to do.

The second test was a test of holiness. Every person who knows the difficulty of gathering a strong core of loyal volunteers knows the fear of splintering, division, and loss. When a leader is attempting to keep his church from "blowing up," it can almost seem right and godly to put up with attacks and gossip and sin.

At this time, there was "sin in the camp" at the church. Everyone knew it, but we all tiptoed around it. An older man with longtime community roots was engaged in character assassination because he could not manipulate or control me or the direction of the church. I tried to arrange a meeting between him and our superintendent for resolution, and he refused. "I don't have a problem with the superintendent," he said. "I have a problem with you."

I tried to ignore the attacks, press on positively, and not make people feel they had to take sides. One day, this man made an error in his phone campaign against me. He dialed a wrong number and, without realizing whom he was talking to, started unloading about his plans for me. It turns out he had inadvertently called a church leader. After hearing what this man said, she immediately called me, weeping, and said, "Dwight—you have to do something." In that moment, God showed me that I had allowed my fear of losing the church to give sin and cowardice an opportunity to flourish all around. At that moment, I decided to call myself and the other church leaders to holy boldness.

I told the woman who had called me, "I have been here in this community for twelve years. If he can sit down over a cup of coffee or in a brief phone call convince someone that I have been evilly misled, there's nothing in the world I can do to change it. My arguments will only add fuel to the fire. One of you has to have the guts, the grace, and the godliness to confront this sin. This is your church, not mine. You'll have to deal with it."

I was at peace with my choice. Regardless of what the church leader did, I knew I had passed the test. But I didn't know what would happen. It seemed likely the church would splinter and lose many people. But God and His people came through. The church leaders took a stand for integrity in our community and told the man he had to leave. In the aftermath of both these tests to obedience, we saw the Acts 2:47 result in our church community: "And the Lord added to their number daily those who were being saved" (NIV).

As I went through these stretching experiences, I felt the fear and pain of struggle, and then the exhilaration of obedience. God was preparing that third test for me.

THE BIGGEST TEST OF ALL

Patty and I had a healthy and happy son, our daughter had just been born, and we were buying a home. I was as content as I had ever hoped to be. I said publicly several times, "If I died today, you could put on my tombstone that I died a happy man."

So often what we say and believe to be true gets tested so we can actually *know* what is true.

After the family spent a summer day together, my sisters expressed concern about a mole on my leg. I laughed it off, but that night I dreamed that my body was full of cancer. I was still very flippant about it all the next day as I asked Patty to make me an appointment with my doctor. I went in for the biopsy, and then we left on vacation. On our return, Patty called the doctor for a report. She hung up the phone and, white faced, said the dreaded word: *malignant*. I needed surgery as soon as possible.

I had always talked like I was a man of faith, but actually I was a man in denial. I cried the whole night before the surgery. I groaned with the longing to live and raise my children. But at the same time, I deeply wanted to be a man like Job. I wanted to be a man who would serve God whether or not He fulfilled my dreams. As the night came to an end, I was able to say to God from my heart, "If I never get to do the rest of the things I want to do, if this will lead to the end for me, I have already been blessed beyond what I deserve. You have done well by me. I can die a blessed man."

God gave me a direct response that tied everything else together in a message of great clarity: "You will not physically die. But if you are going to live the life I require of you, you must die to men's opinions."

The test for me was tailored exactly to what was and still is most likely to bring me down: I am by nature a people pleaser. I want to be liked, even loved. Being misunderstood is my greatest fear. This tendency is the one thing that can most easily cause me to waver, to sin, and to kill my story. Through the test God put me through, I realized that I can't afford to give in to my weakness or excuse it.

Everyone has a specific weakness, a specific threat to his or her story. If we are honest with ourselves, or if we allow a trusted person to be honest with us, we know what those issues are. As Solomon said, "Sensible people will see trouble coming and avoid it, but an unthinking person will walk right into it and regret it later" (Prov. 22:3, author's paraphrase).

Some people fail because of sexual sin. Some people become entrapped by addictions. Others never take control over their financial issues. You might struggle with family issues and let unresolved situations take you off course. Pride may be your downfall and cause you to reject counsel that would spare you pain and loss. Or, like so many, you might lose your spectacular finish through laziness and complacency.

Looking through human eyes, we may see some of these reasons as worse than others. The fact is, in much of Christian society my weakness for people pleasing is considered a good thing. But God knows, Satan knows, and I know that it is not. It is Satan's best weapon for my destruction.

The devil doesn't care *how* he ruins my story; he just wants to diminish all that God has designed for me. That's true for you, too. But the Word urges us to not allow Satan to outsmart us and to be aware of his schemes (see 2 Cor. 2:11). Own the threat to your final chapter being your best, and attack it head-on.

WHAT FINISHING WELL REALLY LOOKS LIKE

Dr. Clinton says that though the exact description of finishing well may vary a bit from leader to leader, there are some common threads among those whose stories end with a spectacular last page. The characteristics Clinton listed include:

1. Maintaining a personal vibrant relationship with God right up to the end.

2. Maintaining a learning posture, and learning from various kinds of sources— life especially.

3. Manifesting Christlikeness, as evidenced by the fruit of their lives.

4. Living out truth, so that convictions and promises of God are real.

5. Leaving behind one or more ultimate contributions.

6. Walking with a growing awareness of a sense of destiny and seeing some or all of it fulfilled.

As I read these characteristics, I see in my mind names and faces of people whose lives got bigger and better as they approached the end of their earthly story. My father is one of those. As I'm writing, he is in his nineties, retired, but still very active in ministry. My mother went to heaven several years ago, finishing exceedingly well, and her death has only tightened Dad's grip on his destiny.

I have committed myself to centering my life around six pillars I have chosen related to these characteristics. The pillars are:

Pillar #1—Relationship. There should never come a day when any*thing* or any*one* becomes more important than our personal relationship with God. Many of us allow our God connection to get its steam from another person, not from our own vigorous faith. Maybe you know someone whose story took a turn like this one: A man appears to be a strong believer who walks faithfully with God—until sometime after his wife dies. As his grief becomes more manageable, he drifts away from God and the church, and after a few years, he is no longer recognizable as anything but a pretty good man. Turns out his faith was always more about being his wife's husband than actually having a vibrant personal relationship with God.

Sadly, some people drift from any of the practices and signs of a vital faith when they are no longer in "professional Christian ministry." That's because their "relationship" with God was more about career and success, so when the recognition and paychecks started coming from a different source, everything about faith looked different, too.

Some of us have a faith that shines brilliantly during a season of life—a season of health strain or huge challenges, or when we are raising the kids, or when we are building the company. But when the situations change, *we* change. It's not that we don't believe anymore. It's just that we are managing differently now. The dependence on God we once felt is lessened—we've "grown up" and "matured," so we just do things differently now.

Whatever the reason, drifting away from absolute dependence on God will diminish your story. That was the point of Jesus' direct instruction, "If you remain in me and I in you, you will bear much fruit; apart from me you can do nothing" (John 15:5 NIV). He didn't say that apart from Him I would accomplish *less* of value—He said I would do *nothing* of value.

Maintaining and building my relationship with the One who loves me most and made me for fellowship with Him must be number one every day of my life. It's not the work I do *for* Him that matters; it's the relationship I have *with* Him.

Pillar #2—Teachability. A successful story brings with it some accompanying dangers. When we enjoy success, others look to us for guidance and help. As we share our expertise and knowledge, over time we become more and more susceptible to arrogance and a closed mind. We can easily begin to feel that we have a lock on life, and there's really not much more we need to learn, especially from any source we did not choose. We trust our own opinions and knowledge more than anything else.

The book of Proverbs leads us toward a life of success, significance, and wisdom. Teachability, humility, and willingness to be corrected are acknowledged as vital ingredients for that life. The writer warns us of the folly of not being teachable, humble, or willing to receive correction:

> *He who corrects a scoffer gets*
> *dishonor for himself,*
> *And he who reproves a wicked*
> *man gets insults for himself.*
> *Do not reprove a scoffer, or he*
> *will hate you,*
> *Reprove a wise man and he*
> *will love you.*
> *Give instruction to a wise man*
> *and he will be still wiser,*
> *Teach a righteous man and*
> *he will increase his learning.*
> Proverbs 9:7–9 NASB

Losing our teachable spirit generally involves pride. When we become "somebody," looking competent and "large and in charge" can become a bigger deal to us than living with integrity. We are not grateful when someone approaches us with some knowledge or concern about our lives. We interpret correction or teaching as an attack, and the end result of that attitude isn't pretty.

A wise man has a very different reaction to being taught or corrected. The people the book of Proverbs repeatedly describes as "wise" are not perfect and they know it. But they are on the right path, and they value the insights of others. They see life's experiences as an opportunity to grow and learn. In contrast to the fool who gives angry insults and retaliation in response to correction, the wise man loves truth and wisdom above all else, so he loves those who give it to him. A wise person cares more about living and finishing well than looking good.

The more I mature, the more willing I am to learn and to receive input and correction. Truly successful people, those who are on the way to finishing well, receive input with a humble, teachable spirit. My goal is to welcome anything that will help me from anyone who will invest in me. Sometimes I bristle a bit at first and feel my defenses rise. But then I remind myself that if I am wise, I will receive even painful input and use it to become wiser still. I've learned that this is the best way to protect my last page.

Pillar #3—Character. If we want to safeguard our stories and make sure they end well, we need to surrender *now* to the work of the Spirit of God in our lives. We need to allow Him to root out the fruit of our sinful natures and to begin growing the fruit of the Spirit in us.

When I was young, one of our neighbors was a bitter, hateful old man. During the summers, he yelled at the neighborhood kids, shook his cane at us as we rode our bikes, and often called the police because he thought we were being too loud.

We expressed our anger to my parents over this, and Dad said, "Oh, please be patient with him. He's a sick old man." My mother quickly and evenly replied, "He didn't get that way because he is old or sick. He's always been that way. As he gets older, he has less and less desire or ability to ever be anything else."

What Mom said about that old man is true for all of us. Our character when we are older is always the result of many daily choices we make throughout our lives. We don't get to be sweet, godly, elderly saints just by getting older. Our choices make us, and we become more of what we really are when we let down our defenses or become less concerned about what people think of us.

The American writer Elbert Hubbard once wrote, "Character is the result of two things: mental attitude and the way we spend our time." When we give our lives to Christ, He expects us to begin thinking like Him, having His attitude, and spending our time with Him. This is how He makes real and lasting change in the way we make choices and behave.

Learning to think like Jesus isn't as impossible as it sounds, because the apostle Paul says we have been given Christ's own mind: "As the scripture says, 'Who knows the mind of the Lord? Who is able to give him advice?' We, however, have the mind of Christ" (1 Cor. 2:16 GNT). As we adopt His way of thinking, we are able to behave like Him. His character becomes our character, so the fruit of the Spirit blossoms in our lives.

Walking with Jesus faithfully and building that relationship daily is like growing a great marriage. Patty and I have been married for twenty-three years now. As we have lived together and loved each other, I have become intimately familiar with her likes and dislikes. I know what she likes to see and hear, and I am deeply aware of what she cares about and what she considers unworthy, insignificant, or worthless. She has also shaped me. As I have walked daily with her, I have learned and grown from her knowledge, responses, joy, and hopes. Her character has become my joy and my character.

In a far more significant way, the goal of my relationship with Jesus is to make me like Him. I pray daily to see my life and possibilities from His perspective. When I spend time with Him, my character becomes more and more a reflection of His. If I am more like Jesus on my last page than anywhere else, my story will end well.

Pillar #4—Truth. For an author's story to end well, he or she has to "keep it real." Over time, it is possible to mouth words and phrases, repeat promises and speak of faith, but lose the reality of our relationship with God. Paul warned his spiritual son Timothy to safeguard himself and his story by having nothing to do with people who act religious or have an appearance of godliness but are disconnected from the power of God (see 2 Tim. 3:5).

I want to immerse myself in the truth of God and then live like I really believe it. I want to live so connected to the truth and reality of the promises of God that certain things about me are predictable. For example, since I know God will supply all my needs according to His riches in glory by Christ Jesus, no matter what the economy does, I will always tithe and be radically generous. Since I know Jesus will never leave me or forsake me, I will never give in to feelings of rejection or abandonment. Since I can do all things as Christ pours His strength through me, I will never pull back from the risks and steps of faith He places in front of me. And since I know that all of God's plans for me are for my good and not evil, I will not give in to despair no matter what happens. I am convinced that my story depends on filling myself with the truth of God and acting on it. I carry a card with me that lists a few dozen scriptures to remind me of the truth of who I am in Christ. I read it every day, sometimes more than that. This is one of the tools I use to continue living in God's truth.

It is easy when I have an opportunity to take a step of obedience that feels risky to talk a bigger game than I play. But when I remind myself of the truth of God—that in Christ I am an overcomer, a victor, secure, accepted, and significant—I have the courage to take the step and live out the promise.

Pillar #5—Contribution. Moses was exposed to more death in his lifetime than I can imagine. As the last living member of the older generation to leave Egypt for the Promised Land, he saw all his peers die in the desert. Several million people perished over the forty-year period of wandering. Psalm 90 is Moses' reflection on the meaning of life. He stresses how short it is and how temporary all things seem to be, and he ends his psalm with a prayer all mankind can understand. He pleads, "God, establish the work of our hands."

You might say it this way: "God, make what I do matter."

It's a human urge. We were created for significance, and we are restless and empty without it. We want to make a contribution that matters and is recognized. We want to make an impact. That's why trophy stores run a brisk business, why award shows attract such attention, and why monuments, large and small, dot cemeteries and parks and city buildings.

I have learned that I must make my decisions not just for today but for beyond my lifetime. I want to make an ultimate contribution, something that lasts beyond my life. The message of Revelation 14:13 is compelling: Those who die in the Lord are unusually blessed. They rest from their labor, but their works keep on working. That's the contribution I seek.

I know that God has called me to deliberately and intentionally build my life for ultimate contributions, starting with those I make in my own family. I want to leave more than a godly heritage. I want my children to leave home with a life of great faith and trust in an all-powerful God. Therefore, Patty and I have to live lives of great faith and trust in an all-powerful God in front of them. I want them to not simply know *about* God but to truly *trust* Him with all of their hearts—with their time, talent, and treasure.

I want my kids to have a truly biblical worldview: God loves all the world; we have been called to make a difference in this world He loves; it is possible to make a difference because of the greatness of God. Patty and I have never set a goal that our children would go into full-time career ministry, but we pray that they each believe that God has a higher purpose and calling on their lives than fulfilling the American dream.

As of this writing, our three oldest all are moving in the direction of some kind of full-time Christian ministry, while the youngest one is still being shaped and molded by his experiences here at home. Howard Hendricks said that if you want people to bleed with passion, you as their leader must hemorrhage. I want our contribution through our children to be enabled because Patty and I lived fully surrendered to God, because our passion for Him bled through all we did and convinced our children that we serve a great God who is fully capable of fulfilling everything He asks them to do.

Pillar #6—Destiny. Alexander Mackay, missionary to the deepest and darkest places in Africa in the mid-1800s, explained his willingness to do what most everyone else considered foolhardy and dangerous: "My heart burns for the deliverance of Africa. . . . What is this you write—'Come home'? Surely now, in our terrible dearth of workers, it is not the time for anyone to desert his post. . . . Man is immortal till his work is done. Use me in Thy service alone, blessed Savior."

God used Mackay as a pioneer-engineer-preacher to build more than 230 miles of road into Uganda from the coast so goods and the Gospel could be transported. In the fourteen years he served before his death, he also translated Matthew's Gospel into the language of the people. He was fearless because he had a sense that God's hand was on him. He would not step out from under the protection of obedience to God, but in that place he felt safe to do whatever God said. He was a man of destiny.

People who finish their stories with a spectacular page, those who claim the victory of the overcomer, do it with a sense of destiny. That's why the apostle Paul looked forward with such anticipation. He did not fear defeat or disaster but pressed forward toward the prize. He could do that because he sensed God's call of destiny.

I intend to finish well. I feel a kinship with Jeremiah the prophet, who wrote:

> *The word of the* LORD *came to me, saying, "Before I formed you in the womb I knew you, before you were born I set you apart; I appointed you as a prophet to the nations." "Alas, Sovereign* LORD," *I said, "I do not know how to speak; I am too young." But the* LORD *said to me, "Do not say, 'I am too young.' You must go to everyone I send you to and say whatever I command you. Do not be afraid of them, for I am with you and will rescue you," declares the* LORD. *Then the* LORD *reached out his hand and touched my mouth and said to me, "I have put my words in your mouth. See, today I appoint you over nations and kingdoms to uproot and tear down, to destroy and over-throw, to build and to plant."*
> JEREMIAH 1:4–10 NIV

I am humbled and empowered because I know in the deepest part of my heart that before I was born, God planned for me. He set me apart and appointed me for this time and place. I have a destiny! I never need to fear going anywhere or doing anything or speaking any word God commands me. I have no reason to fear because He is with me and will rescue me. It won't be over until He says it is over. I wake up every morning with that sense of destiny.

This is not just about me. God wants every single story to be great. He not only is not willing for anyone to perish, but He wants each of us to be works of art: "For we are God's handiwork, created in Christ Jesus to do good works, which God prepared in advance for us to do" (Eph. 2:10 NIV).

God wants you to write an amazing lifelong story, and He wants your very last page to be your best.

Only God can work with you to make that happen. Only He can help you to write your personal "only God" story, a story that can and will change your own corner of the world.

"A MAGNA CARTA OF TRUST BY AN OUT-OF-CONTROL DISCIPLE"
by Leonard Sweet

I am part of the Church of the Out-of-Control. I once was a control junkie, but now am an Out-of-Control Disciple. I've given up my control to God. I trust and obey the Spirit. I've jumped off the fence, I've stepped over the line, I've pulled out all the stops, I'm holding nothing back. There's no turning back, looking around, slowing down, backing away, letting up, or shutting up. It's life against the odds, outside the box, over the wall, the game of life played without goal lines other than "Thy Will Be Done..."

I'm done lapdogging for the topdogs, the wonderdogs, the overdogs, or even the underdogs. I'm done playing according to the rules, whether it's Robert's Rules of Order or Miss Manner's Rules of Etiquette or Martha Stewart's Rules of Living or Louis Farrakhan's Rules of America's Least Wanted or Merrill Lynch's money-minding/ bottom-lining/ladder-climbing Rules of America's Most Wanted.

I am not here to please the dominant culture or to serve any all-show/no-go bureaucracies. I live to please my Lord and Savior. My spiritual taste buds have graduated from fizz and froth to fire and ice.

Sometimes I'm called to sharpen the cutting edge, and sometimes to blunt the cutting edge. Don't give me that old-time religion. Don't give me that new-time religion. Give me that all-time religion that's as hard as rock and as soft as snow.

I've stopped trying to make life work, and started trying to make life sing. I'm finished with secondhand sensations, third-rate dreams, low-risk high-rise trades and goose-stepping, flag-waving crusades. I no longer live by and for anything but everything God-breathed, Christ-centered, and Spirit-driven.

I can't be bought by any personalities or perks, positions, or prizes. I won't give up, though I will give in. . .to openness of mind, humbleness of heart, and generosity of spirit. When shorthanded and hard-pressed, I will never again hang in there. I will stand in there, I will run in there, I will pray in there, I will sacrifice in there, I will endure in there—in fact I will do everything in there but hang. My face is upward, my feet are forward, my eyes are focused, my way is cloudy, my knees are worn, my seat un-creased, my heart burdened, my spirit light, my road narrow, my mission wide.

I won't be seduced by popularity, traduced by criticism, by hypocrisy, or trivialized by mediocrity. I am organized religion's best friend, and worst nightmare. I won't back down, slow down, shut down, or let down until I'm preached out, teached out, healed out, or hauled out of God's mission in the world entrusted to members of the Church of the Out-of-Control. . .to unbind the confined, whether they're the downtrodden or the up-scale, the overlooked or the underrepresented.

My fundamental identity is as a disciple of Jesus—but even more, as a disciple of Jesus who lives in Christ, who doesn't walk through history simply "in His steps," but seeks to travel more deeply IN HIS SPIRIT. Until He comes again or calls me home, you can find me filling, not killing, time so that one day He will pick me out in the lineup of the ages as one of His own. And then. . .it will be worth it all. . .to hear these words, the most precious words I can ever hear: "Well done, thou good and faithful Out-of-Control Disciple."

ACTION STEPS

1. Spend time critically thinking out the rest of your life.

2. Focus on the six pillars: Relationship, Teachability, Character, Truth, Contribution, and Destiny. Write your own "destiny document," a plan of action for keeping your story on track for an "only God" story all the way through.

{ My last page to you. . . }

Thank you for reading this book. I hope God has spoken to you through it. I want to say three final things that I hope will encourage and motivate your next step.

First, start writing an "only God" story where you are. Today. Right now. Don't wait.

> When I was a young man, I wanted to change the world. I found it was difficult to change the world, so I tried to change my nation. When I found I couldn't change the nation, I began to focus on my town. I couldn't change the town and as an older man, I tried to change my family. Now, as an old man, I realize the only thing I can change is myself, and suddenly I realize that if long ago I had changed myself, I could have made an impact on my family. My

> *family and I could have made an impact on*
> *our town. Their impact could have changed*
> *the nation, and I could indeed have changed*
> *the world.*
> AUTHOR UNKNOWN

Second, never be put off by temporary discouragements. Think of God's dream of writing the story of redemption through Jesus. Satan attempted to thwart it by convincing Herod to kill the baby boys. Peter, one of Jesus' own followers, tried to stop Jesus from obediently going to the cross. People who should have been cooperating with Jesus were pulling back and denying Him. The Crucifixion appeared to be the biggest failure of all, and it turned out to be the world's greatest victory story of all time. Don't let appearances deceive you. God's stories always end in victory. You may spend some days in grief, but get over it. Your "only God" story is the treasure in the field. Sacrifice anything to get it.

Last, I want to pray with you, for both of us.

Almighty God, Author of life and all good things,

I pray that we would see Your greatness and know that nothing is too hard or difficult for You. May we never forget that You are alive, powerful, gracious, and merciful. May we move past our doubts to know with certainty that You are willing and able to move in a fresh way in our lives, Your church, and Your world.

I pray that we would see Your goodness, that You will not withhold any good thing from those who walk uprightly, that we would know that You are not only able to help, but that it is Your pleasure to help us.

I pray that we would trust You with all of our hearts and lean not on our own understandings, but that in all of our ways we would acknowledge You, knowing that You will direct our paths.

I pray that from Your glorious, unlimited resources, You will empower us with inner strength through Your Spirit. I ask that Christ will make His home in our hearts as we trust in Him. May our roots grow down into Your love and keep us strong. And may we have the power to understand, as all Your people should, how wide, how long, how high, and how deep Your love is. May we experience the love of Christ, though it is too great to understand fully. Then we will be made complete with all the fullness of life and power that comes from You, and all fear will be cast out.

I pray that You would guard our hearts, for out of them flow the issues of life. Help us stay away from every appearance of evil, and train ourselves to be godly, fully useable vessels in Your hand.

I pray that You would give us courage to make bold, decisive calls that challenge ourselves as well as others to follow Your ways with conviction and clarity. May we be willing to risk our lives to gain that which we can never lose.

I pray that You would give us the wisdom of the Spirit that surpasses that of Solomon. Help us see as You see, and then do what You say.

I pray that we would be authentic, genuine, and vulnerable, so that it would be clear to all that the greatness of our stories is because of Your faithfulness.

I pray that each of us will finally be able to say as Paul said, head high and spirit undaunted: "I have fought the fight, I have run the race, I have kept the faith."

In the name of the one and only God I pray,

Amen.

DECLARATION OF PERSONAL RESPONSIBILITY
by Danny Cox

- I currently possess everything I've truly wanted and deserved. This is based on what I have handed out to date. My possessions, my savings, and my lifestyle are an exact mirror of me, my efforts, and my contribution to society. What I give, I get. If I am unhappy with what I have received, it is because, as yet, I have not paid the required price. I have lingered too long in the "quibbling stage."

- I fully understand that time becomes a burden to me only when it is empty. The past is mine, and at this very moment I am purchasing another twenty-four hours of it. The future quickly becomes the past at a control point called the present moment. I not only truly live at that point, but I have full responsibility for the highest and best use of the irreplaceable now.

- I accept full responsibility for both the successes and failures in my life. If I am not what I desire to be at this point, what I am is my compromise. I no longer choose to compromise with my undeveloped potential.

- I am the sum total of the choices I have made, and I continue to choose daily. What I now put under close scrutiny is the value of each upcoming choice. Therein lies the quality of my future lifestyle.

- Will my future belong to the "old me" or the "new me"? The answer depends on my attitude toward personal growth at this very moment. What time is left is all that counts, and that remaining time is my responsibility. With a newfound maturity I accept full

responsibility for how good I can become at
what is most important to me.

With personal growth comes a fear of
the unknown and new problems. Those
problems are nothing more than the
expanding shadow of my personal growth. I
now turn my very real fear, with God's help,
into a very real adventure.

- My life now expands to meet my newfound
destiny. "Old me" meet the "new me."

 **Dwight Mason** has been lead pastor of NewPointe Community Church since 1985. NewPointe is a thriving and growing group of more than 3,500 people across multiple locations in Northeast Ohio.